WOMEN CRUSHING MEDIOCRITY

Presented by Dr. Cheryl Wood

ISBN: 978-1-7923-6670-3
Kindle ISBN: 978-1-7923-6671-0

Women Crushing Mediocrity

Introduction
By Dr. Cheryl Wood

Visionary of Women Crushing Mediocrity

13x Best-Selling Author | International Empowerment Speaker | TEDx Speaker | Speaker Development Coach | Leadership Expert

Women are powerful beyond all measure! I say that boldly and confidently as a witness to the fact that women from all walks of life and backgrounds repeatedly demonstrate the strength to crush mediocrity in every aspect of life. I have watched women courageously press through, persevere, and thrive in the face of the very things that were meant to break them. I have witnessed women toss their fears, doubts, and apprehension to the wayside in order to explore new possibilities and soar beyond being average in their lives. I have witnessed women crush anything that stands in their way and threatens to keep them in an 'existence' versus fully living life. And every time I see such a powerful display of willpower and determination, I am deeply moved and inspired. From my perspective, there is nothing greater than seeing a woman decide, through her actions, not just her words, what her life will be instead of allowing her life to be dictated by circumstances or other people.

One thing is for sure – every woman has a story of crushing mediocrity that deserves to be told! And Women Crushing Mediocrity is created to give you an exclusive opportunity to "hear" some of those personal stories of women who refuse to be held hostage to ordinary. I celebrate each of the co-authors who have stepped up to share their stories as a part of this transformative project because they acknowledge that their story is "about them but not for them." There is truly unparalleled power in sharing your story to bless someone else!

Women Crushing Mediocrity is by women for women. As you immerse yourself into each of the stories, I hope it serves as a potent reminder that you are destined for greatness and that you owe it to yourself to step out into the deep to explore what else is possible for you. It is my hope that Women Crushing Mediocrity will reignite the fire within you to be AMAZING – which is your birthright – not just ordinary and to develop a commitment to crush anything that stands in your way of creating a life that you're in love with.

In my personal journey, I have had to consistently crush mediocrity – in my own thinking, in my expectations of what was possible, in my belief systems – in order to walk fully in my divine purpose. As I have continued to crush mediocrity, it has positioned me to become more confident, driven, determined, and tenacious in sharing my voice, using my gifts, and making my mark in the world instead of simply staying quiet and accepting whatever life hands me. I have become more aware and confident about who I am and whose I am and more conscious of the need to play all out in life. Most importantly, crushing mediocrity in my own life has allowed me to serve as a vessel to equip, empower, and inspire other women globally to develop new levels of confidence in their own lives and come to the front of the room to share their voice and their gifts. After all, our lives should always be bigger than ourselves. And that's the belief system that each co-author in this project holds strongly – that their life is bigger than themselves and that their greatest impact in the world will always stem from sharing their authentic stories, experiences, and life lessons.

As you take a deep dive into the stories shared in Women Crushing Mediocrity, it is our hope that you will feel inspired, enlightened, reenergized, and reignited for the impact and legacy you are meant to create in the world. It is our deep hope that you will be reminded of your own strength to crush mediocrity and to dream a little bigger, fight a little harder for what you want, bounce back a little quicker when you get knocked down, and to never ever give up. You were not created to be ordinary; you were designed to be EXTRAordinary!

Dr. Cheryl Wood
Visionary of Women Crushing Mediocrity
WEBSITE: www.cherylempowers.com
EMAIL: info@cherylwoodempowers.com
SOCIAL MEDIA: @CherylEmpowers

Stephanie Barnes

Is Your Bank Vault Empty?
By Stephanie Barnes

Does a bank robber rob an empty bank? The first time those words were deposited into my spirit, I heard them, but they truly didn't resonate until some time later. Hey, Steff, a thief (typically seeking to steal something of "VALUE") doesn't rob an empty bank. Think about that for a minute. WOW, lightbulb moment, right? As I reflect back over my life as a woman of color, victim of domestic violence and recovering drug addiction, I had no clue as to why I was being so challenged, but yet preserved as a living testimony for such a time as this. See, I'm an only child on my mom's side, and talking about being spoiled! So, as I developed into adulthood, when I felt rejected about something (but was really being protected by prayer) my mindset was, "God doesn't love me like He loves others", and the crazy part was, I grew up in the church, so I knew better. But me being me, I was in a hurry and wanted to do things my way. I wanted what I wanted, and I'd felt since God was either taking too long (for me) or wasn't going to give me what I thought I needed at the time, I would just go out and get it done myself ~ Steff's way. After all, I was good at what I did. You see, I could talk people in and out of something or a situation. Not so much of something terribly bad, but let's just say I benefited from it in the end. I thought I had it all under control, but still something wasn't right. I couldn't seem to get that one opportunity that I so desired in life, leaving me to ponder "What's wrong with me? I'm approachable, cute, fashionable dresser, independent, a people person, and that's just to name a few. Arrogant? Far from it! But being talked down to and called names that questioned my confidence, out of the same mouth (of my abuser's) that said they'd love me forever-unconditionally.. I have to love up on me being my #1 fan and inspire my insecurities to ensure it stays #StampedSOLID. For some reason, in particular, men with their own business were typically the ones to step up and pursue me, ensuring I took notice of them, even to this day. So, I've always had an entrepreneurial business mindset. I was engaged, but didn't get married; my bank account was cute, but a few millions sure looks cuter; my health – pretty good, but I could work on some areas to make it better. So, I had to question myself, "What is it Steff? Why does it feel like there's more in you beyond what's considered "Average"? What's instilled in you? What or Who is God molding and preserving you for?"

As I reflect back, I could've been taken from this Earth a long time ago. Especially the time I was forced to the floor with a silver 9 millimeter pistol temporarily tattooed to my temple by a man that was paranoid and high on cocaine. At any instant, with the pull of a trigger, it could've been over for me. Him making a decision to take the one thing my mom cherishes the most, but God sent a protective shield to intervene.. "Not yet, it's not her time." After being delivered from my addiction, Grace and Mercy became more evident to me. I'm supposed to be here. There's something God wants me to do. I'd even experienced loss of employment 2 years apart from each other with a mortgage and other financial responsibilities, that could've mentally took me out of here, while living as a single woman with no hubby to turn to or generational inheritance to tap into to make it all better. However, did I lack one day without the basic necessities of life? By the Grace of God, I did not, but let's keep the facts realistic. I'm not going to dress it up as if it was easy to get through. Yes, there were tears, doubt, fear, shame, anger, and a few cuss words of frustration, but when I got a grip of my mindset and repented, I finally let go of my EGO (Easing God Out) deciding that enough was enough. That's when God stepped in and let me know that the battle was not mines to fight, it's His. I learned this the hard way. He does the supernatural and impossible so that He'll get the Glory, and my job is to do the possible by showing up, listen for His instructions of obedience so I can live victoriously.

Are you familiar with the scripture, "Life and death are in the power of the tongue?" (Proverbs 18: 21) The same verbal weapon I used back then for selfish influences, I'm now using that same verbal weapon to inspire and motivate others.

It didn't hit me until age 50, when my first co-authored book was published that my name is not allowed to align or be in the same sentence of being "Average or Mediocre", and the only credit I give my past is that it built me to be who I am today. #IB4T. If my bank vault was empty, and I had nothing of "VALUE" that other women couldn't benefit from, a spiritual thief wouldn't come in any form to try to rob me of my passion and God's purpose. God has something greater for us, and the moment we overcome our do-it-yourself mental distractions, limited beliefs and fear, the sooner we begin to walk into our greater purpose of being an unstoppable force.

Regardless of what stage you're at in life, when your "enough is enough" arrives at your door, invite it in, look yourself in the mirror, and thank yourself for showing up. Affirm It & Own It! My Bank Vault is Not Empty & I Am a "Woman Crushing Mediocrity".

Bio:

I'm a Washington, DC native devoted to authenticity, as anyone who has met me can attest. As a victim and advocate of Domestic & Drug Abuse, I use my voice to influence and inspire women that are ready to break through their silence. As a co-author of Pray, Pursue, Persist and the Proprietor of Global Vision Productions, my goal is to make meaningful connections with audiences of diverse backgrounds as I have an insatiable appetite for helping others maximize their potential. Spending time with God is my top priority, traveling across the country exploring various cultures is my sobriety-mental reset, and embracing smooth sounds of music soothes my soul.

Dedications: Rosa Barnes (Mother), Samuel Armstrong (Father-Deceased), Maehalie Barnes (92 Years Young Nana), Delma Parks (Aunt, Spiritual Advisor-Deceased) and a host of family and friends.

Website: www.globalvisionprod.com
Facebook & Instagram: @globalvisionprod
Email: globalvisionprod@gmail.com
Member: National Network to End Domestic Violence [NNEDV]

Debra Bell-Campbell

Released
By Debra Bell-Campbell

"No One Can Make You Feel Inferior Without Your Consent"
Eleanor Roosevelt

Have you ever found yourself feeling less-than, inadequate, or afraid? It may not be you, but it certainly was me for a long time. I spent many of my adult years clawing my way from under my siblings' shadows. This wasn't an easy feat as I had seven older sisters and brothers to look up to, compare to, and follow behind. Would they ever know that I never felt as if I mattered? I was number eight of twelve; seven above me and four below me. Everyone needed something.

Their shadows were formidable, yet I persevered as I carved out my niche. Once I emerged as a college graduate, I began to focus my energy on fixing people. Notice, I did not say helping. I hid behind my fears of who I was supposed to be. I camouflaged myself as a therapist and went to work. When I discovered what I was doing garnered results, the pursuit to fix dissipated, and I truly began to facilitate healing. Even at that juncture, I was not fully convinced that I was the catalyst. Self-doubt hovered over me like Superman's kryptonite.

I spent a large portion of my life masquerading in fear, seeking one more certification, one more piece of paper to define my KSAs (knowledge, skills, and abilities). 2 Timothy 1:7 says, "For God hath not given us the spirit of fear, but of power." I wore a cloak of invisibility for many years, but that's a whole other chapter in another book. Suddenly, I was forced to release the cloak and come to the realization that, "Yes, I can," was more than a slogan.

Tonia M. Blackwood

Destroying Mediocrity Mindset... Legacy Prevails
By Tonia M. Blackwood

To start, let's take a hard look at the word 'mediocrity.' The dictionary defines it as the "quality or state of being mediocre." Well, what is mediocre? Words that come to mind include ordinary, common-place, adequate, passable, sufficient, and basic. Let me stress up front that I am no authority on the topic of how to be mediocre. However, I believe the obvious question to ask is do you think these words correctly define who you are? Since you're reading this book, it is safe to assume you don't.

If you're okay using these words to describe your life journey, then more power to you! Most people naturally cringe at words like those being used to describe anything about them. Not because we think so highly of ourselves, but because we can feel a swelling of rebellion in our belly simply at the implication. Personally, it goes against everything poured into me and my siblings; seeds planted by legacy-building parents.

You see, my parents came to the United States from a small country called Panama, located in Central America. Panama is a small, narrow country smack dab in between Costa Rica and Colombia and home to one of the Seven Wonders of the World, the Panama Canal. My parents did not come to the United States together. It was quite a different journey for both of them. My father came seeking the "American Dream," but my mother was sent here to live with relatives

24

to put plenty of distance between her and the man she hoped to marry one day. The roads that brought them together were bumpy, divisive, and challenging but God had a plan! Their incredible union brought six remarkably similar, yet different personalities into this world.

What was important during those formative years? We were taught to appreciate the little things in life. Keeping our family together; building something that would last, and most importantly, never ever giving up! These are the Blackwood family principles! My father was a hardworking blue-collar guy, part-time entrepreneur, and dreamer; and my mother was the nurturer and realistic planner. Together, they made the perfect combination to create a brood of children allergic to mediocrity!

We weren't raised in the church, but the underlying current of who God is was never lost on us. We were what some would call CEO (Christmas, Easter, & Other) Christians. If not faith, what accounted for such a strong work ethic and positive disposition? I'm convinced it was my mother's sheer determination to ensure her six children had structure and a home to call their own. There was also my father's perseverance and willingness to work several jobs while running a t-shirt business. There was always a clear understanding of the sacrifices our parents made to safeguard our success. There were no excuses, just the desire to make them proud and collectively contribute to our family legacy. The foundation was laid. Work hard at everything you do and if someone says something can't be done, crush it anyway!

How does a young lady with that type of inherited fortitude lose her way? How does she end up on academic probation her freshman year of college? Newfound freedom? Maybe being separated from family, having a lukewarm faith walk, or experiencing the rude awakening of making my own way in the world caused me to forget all the late hours, close calls, and the sacrifices made to shape me and my siblings.

25

To remedy this, I decided to make a bold, "non-mediocre" move and enlist in the United States Army Reserve. In those days, the firstborn daughter of a Hispanic family enrolling in the military was not exactly a dream come true for immigrant parents. My naysayers, surprisingly some of whom were family, were sure that my childhood asthma, and let's say my "feminine ways," would cause me to fail. However, against all the odds I successfully completed my training. It turned out that taking the extraordinary route had started to become my signature move.

Crushing Mediocrity is a Mindset!

On several occasions I've been told what I shouldn't do, but it has never stopped me from pursuing what God has for me. That is key! A hard lesson I learned over the years [that remains a stumbling block to this day] is that there can be no crushing without checking in with the "Big Guy" upstairs.

That sense of surety in your spirit that tells you, "I got this!" comes from two sources. First, that level of confidence is most often God-given and ties directly to the Heavenly Father's plans for your life. Not everyone is blessed with a cheering committee to build them up and ignite a level of urgency that positions them to conquer every task given, but God is faithful to everyone. Secondly, the seeds that were planted in you, either during your childhood years or in other life experiences have value. You must understand that you were a warrior from day one!

Some may say that being diagnosed with Bell's Palsy and a tumor within an 18-month window should have stopped me, but it did not! Quitting never was and never will be an option! The same can be said about the two brain aneurysms that followed. The decision to get up should be a given! However, how long you stay down, or whether or not you even try to RISE is what counts! This is a mindset shift that many never make. When you have a crushing mediocrity mindset, you cannot afford to stop at ordinary. The many that have gone before you or the opportunity to be the first should ignite a fire in you to surpass limitations. Crushing a mediocre mindset is critical to living an empowered life. It is the first and possibly the most important step. Without it, your world would be very basic indeed!

Bio:

Tonia M. Blackwood, CEO of Then I Rise Enterprises, LLC, is a seasoned professional with 25+ years of corporate & entrepreneurial experience in talent acquisition, marketing, business, and sales. As a Certified Life Coach and Business Strategist, she helps women identify and activate their purpose. She is devoted to impacting lives by providing training and coaching to those who want to take their lives and/or business to the next level. Having successfully walked through what some would consider halting life challenges, Tonia has learned to turn her pain to power and helps her clients reclaim their confidence. She is also a best-selling contributing author and successful podcaster. She holds a bachelors' degree in Management Studies with a concentration in Human Resources, an associate's degree in Business Administration, and a certificate in Women Entrepreneurship from Cornell University. Find out more about this natural cultivator of gifts and talents at www.thenirise.org

27

Delia Butler

How I Crushed Divorce and Conquered Healing Me
By Master Life Coach Delia Butler

I was married two times. Once at 19 and the other at 25 years old. After two marriages, two divorces, and several failed relationships proceeding them, I know that I am an expert on life after divorce.

I'll start by saying I was too young for marriage at those ages. I did not really understand what love was or the amount of work it really took to keep a marriage without being selfish. Looking back to when I was 19, I simply wanted to get out of my mother's house. (REAL TALK!) My first husband was too controlling for me. He was 12-13 years older than me.

After the first marriage, I realized I was not happy. I was young, immature, and selfish (Real Talk.) About six months to a year into that marriage I realized, "Hmmmmm... I think I've made a big mistake." Not necessarily because of him, but rather who I was. I didn't know what to do next.

I remember what my mom said to me when I came to her about no longer wanting to be married. I will never forget her response, "You made your bed, so you have to lay in it!" from the very person I needed in my corner. I felt like I did not have any support at all! Because of this I stayed married another three years being unhappy.. It was a very lonely place to be especially since I felt I had no one there for me. After a while of feeling depressed, trapped, and disappointed in myself, I started talking to and even hanging out with other men because I no longer wanted to be in my marriage, but I didn't really know how to get out of it, and I felt guilty.

After a few years, I left the Island of St. Thomas, where I was born and raised, and came to Maryland to start over with my seven year-old daughter. I had no job, but I had a place to live with my aunty.

When I left the islands, I was 22 years old, still married, but acting single. I finally got a temp job and about six months later, I landed a great, full-time job as an accounting clerk. That is where I met my second husband. I divorced the first one, and eight months later I remarried the second one! (What the hell was I thinking?) I realized I really didn't like being single, and I felt I needed someone to take care of me!

I realized that even though he was ten years older than me, when it came to relationships, I was more mature than him because he wasn't married before, so he depended on me a lot for guidance. That was a big mistake!

When we met, it was a whirlwind romance, and soon after that we married because I became pregnant.

During the 22 years in my second marriage, I didn't feel loved like I thought I was going to experience, which was a total let down. I was gasping for air what seemed like every day. I didn't have any true examples of what a successful marriage looked like.

After years of ups and downs, after both my children were grown and left home, I thought, 'Hey, let me ask my then-husband to rebuild our marriage. I remember that conversation all too well. I approached him on January 1, 2012. I was so excited and ready to start over, put all I could into our marriage, and move forward with positivity. He said "Yes, let's do it!"

Only three months later I found out that he was in a full-blown relationship with someone else! He said he was in love with her, and the relationship had been going on for two years. I was totally devastated to say the least! I truly did not see it coming! Our marriage got negative, ugly, hurtful, angry and confused, so I decided to walk away. Why? You cannot fight for someone when they genuinely believe that they are in love with someone else. Plus, I tried. This fact only hurt me more because of the rejection!

I finally left my house and everything behind! It became pretty bad. I was always in a state of disbelief, like I was in an episode of the Twilight Zone.

Finally, I got my breakthrough after coming to a place of acceptance, forgiveness, and self-love. I created a program for myself after intense research on how to move on from a devastating divorce. I learned that I must break the chain of the past and rebuild my "life after divorce."

I took my life and happiness seriously, and I learned how to get in tune with my feminine energy. I took the mask off and became real with myself; no more pretending to be happy, no more pretending that my marriage was good, no more pretending that everything is going to be ok when I had no control over such things.

To successfully move on from a divorce, forgiveness is critical! I cannot stress that enough. Not just for the other person, but for you. Stop playing around, get serious about healing, and do what you genuinely want with your life.

There's hope after divorce, so rise up, take control of your life, forgive, and do the work necessary to get to your next level, whatever that may be for you.

Let's go!

Bio:

Master Life Coach, better known as Coach Delia! I was born and raised in St. Thomas, Virgin Islands. I have two children and five grandchildren who are my world! I am the Director of Admissions for a private foster care agency, and I opened a private homeless shelter for women and children in 2006-2009.

After a 25 year marriage, I have been single for nearly a decade. I am a Certified Master Life and Professional Life Coach, specializing in life after divorce. I help women transition forward with grace, confidence, and empowerment, allowing them to embrace the newest chapter of their lives.

My goal is to help women grow while remaining agile enough to handle whatever life throws at them. Let me help you take your life to the next level with my programs!

Follow me!

Facebook: @elevationcoachdelia
Instagram: @coachdeliab
LinkedIn: @delia-butler-a70913140

Kearn Crockett Cherry

Lead Like a Champion
By Kearn Crockett Cherry

Greatness is not found in a person who's comfortable. Greatness is found in champions. How often do we hear the best athletes talk about how many hours, days, and months they spend preparing for a single event or game? Many of them still feel like they could do better. They can always see how they can improve their talent. Champions are never satisfied with being average. They are on a mission to crush mediocrity.

You should strive to crush everything set before you like a champion. Over the years, being in business has taught me that you can never simply do enough to get by. Striving to be average is not the road to greatness. When you lead from greatness, the champion will prevail.

After over two decades of business experience, I realized that I would never survive just being average. I couldn't just do business as usual. People who operate businesses by doing just enough always struggle. This includes in personal life and community as well. Mediocrity should never be acceptable.

There was a little girl that I knew who always felt out of place. She was not raised with money, and she was not one of the popular kids. She usually walked through school unnoticed. She stepped up to the challenge of maintaining great grades but not to the point of being a standout. She remained low key throughout her school years, not really having a voice. She carried that into her early adult life, suffering some setbacks. She did what was expected, spending many years working

36

hard and being a provider for her family. Then came a point when she and her husband had to make a decision. They could keep working two to three jobs to provide for their three little kids or they could head off to college while still working. At the time, they did not live near family so they could only depend on each other. This was a risk because they really couldn't afford it, it was time to stop doing what is expected and take a leap of faith.

That little girl was me. Looking back, I realize that we did the unthinkable, but we did it. My husband and I had to make a change. We had been on a deadend cycle of mediocrity or worse. We realized we had to do something bold and risky to change our future, and we did just that. Were there sacrifices? Yes! There were many. I often worried that my three children would suffer because of our decision because they wouldn't get to spend time with their parents, but I did not want them to spend most of their childhood without. We had to teach them that sometimes life included taking risks. We had to set the example that one cannot live in fear and settle for mediocrity. My husband and I knew that we were called for something greater. We knew that it would require us to put in extra hours, days, and months to set our course to greatness. At the end of the day, in order to be a champion, you must never rest before the finish line. There's no mountain too high to climb. There's no goal that is out of reach. It may take a bit longer and require more work, but being comfortable with mediocrity is never an option.

Today, that patience and determination has allowed us to operate our businesses with the same zeal. We learned to be patient by going through trials, tribulations, and taking risks but never settling. You will see that sometimes what needs to be done is not easy. In fact, most times it is pretty hard! A challenge, to me, is "music to my ears" because it gives me the energy to drive even harder. I have the same mindset when working in my community. If there's a need or something missing, I do not wait for someone else to get it done. I take

37

the initiative myself. As far as those three little kids, one is a successful businessman, one is a medical doctor, and the other one is a dentist.

To be a champion, you must seek to dominate anything you do. Never settle to just be average. Always seek to Crush Mediocrity.

Bio:

Kearn Crockett Cherry is called the "Butts in the Seats Queen". She is a speaker, coach, entrepreneur, and #1 Bestselling author. She teaches on "Creating Your Own Profitable Event" especially virtual. She is the co-owner of PRN Home Care for over 24 years while in healthcare over 30 years. She is co-founder and director of Success Women's Conference with over 17,000 virtually. She is the founder of Power Up Summit and Level Up Virtual Summit. Mrs. Cherry is the visionary author for her book anthologies - "Make It Happen" and "Trailblazers Who Lead" I & II. She is co-author of "Women Inspiring Nations" Vol. 2. She has been featured twice in Essence Magazine as the "Comeback Queen". She often says "When one door is close try the next one, if it's close go around to the back, if not Create Your OWN, but never give up."

Walda Collins

Unleash The Warrior In You
By Walda Collins

"The most common way people give up their power is by thinking they don't have any."
Alice Walker

You are exceptional! You are outstanding! You are extraordinary! I know what it's like to live life fearful, timid, and careless. I know what it feels like to feel lost and purposeless. Yet, I also know what it's like to be bold, courageous, strategic and intentional. I came to a cross-road of having to make a decision that would affect the rest of my life. Afraid of being swayed in the direction of commonality, I kept it a secret, at least until I was sure of my decision. With three younger siblings trailing behind me, I wanted to relieve my mother, who had raised five children alone, of the burden of caring for me. I did what I thought was best. The decision I made released me from difficulties and negativity in order to embrace my power within. My journey is about challenge, change, and commitment.

While it was heartbreaking to depart from family and friends, the time had come for me to leave that which was comfortable and head to a place of unfamiliarity. At the ripe, young age of 19 years old, I was stripped of my inadequacies, forced to let go of my civilian identity, and thrust into the unknown to fight for my life. I met a "me" that I didn't even know existed. I forged physical, mental, and moral toughness in the day-to-day grind. Oftentimes, I wanted to surrender to the pain, but the push inside helped me to endure. Beyond the pain, the battle of who I was- a shy, timid, young girl,- and who I was

40

becoming- ignited, a fearless flame, and arrested the struggle within. Moments of intensity and battles of exhaustion birthed one of the nation's most elite warriors. I was now a United States Marine.

Much like a diamond, it often takes intense heat and a collision with purpose to find the potential and power you already possess. I've come to know warriors don't make excuses, they build expectations. They possess a deliberate expectation to succeed. Warriors understand that before we ever birth anything, there will be a battle. I had to endure the rigors of growing, learning, pushing, and pulling to complete this journey. The battle was 99 percent mental. The mind is powerful. Our thoughts, expectations, and attitudes start in the mind.

Over the thirteen weeks of my life transformation, I developed an attitude. No, not the kind you're thinking of. It was an attitude of winning. I was being transformed, and my mind was being renewed. I had no idea I was being called, anointed, and appointed for my due season. I only knew that I was determined to fulfill this endeavor, and nothing was going to stop me. Were there challenges? Yes! Did it bring about change? Absolutely! Was I committed? To the end, my friend! The set up was all in God's plan.

I didn't realize it yet, but I was stepping into my greatness as I welcomed the challenge, embraced change, and travailed in my commitment. After so many years of succumbing to worldly ways rather than standing on my own, I realized that I was different. After I answered the call, I knew it was time to break away from the social norms and rise above mediocrity. Little did I know, I'd face the challenge of a lifetime. You know you've been challenged when trials and tribulations test you beyond your perceived ability. You know you've met the challenge when you've stood boldly and defied the odds that confront you. Without challenges, we can't grow. If you're never challenged, you'll never change. Challenges awaken our brilliance and ignite our propensity for change.

The two secrets to embracing change and pressing through mediocrity are resilience and flexibility. Resilience embodies the mental toughness that one is forced to build when faced with adversity. Flexibility manifests the capacity to bounce back and shift directions when encountering road blocks. Warriors are strong, resilient, and flexible. That which doesn't stop them only brings out their purpose. We often despise change. Why? Because it shakes us out of our comfort zone, and thrusts us into the unpredictable. Change can be a painful, slow process or an abrupt jolt from our slothful slumber. It was change that allowed me to walk in boldness and leave behind paralyzing fear and doubt. It was change that revealed the power I possessed inside. It was change that pushed me towards intentionality, and it was change that showed me how to be strategic. Don't fear change. Allow it to propel you past your pain and push you into your potential, power, and purpose. Change in itself is powerful. We must break through the limiting belief that we are in any way inferior. Change transpires through our mindset. Changing the way we think ultimately changes our lives. Change unleashes our aspirations and guides our commitments to remain steadfast.

Can you remember a time when you wanted something so bad but you couldn't commit to what it took to obtain it? I've had many goals and dreams that I wanted to attain but lost focus, lost hope, or just plain lacked commitment. I've missed way too many opportunities, and so have you, but there's still hope. It's not too late to get involved; impact a life or even rock the boat. It's time for you to stand in the face of adversity and commit yourself to your cause. You must have a "no matter what" mentality. Dreams are just dreams, and goals are just an idea until you've made a commitment to act upon them. Commitment motivates you to remain devoted to your dreams. Challenge, change, and commitment will unleash the warrior in you!

Bio:
Walda Collins served over 23 years of honorable service in the U.S. Marine Corps. For eight years, Walda was the Executive Chef and

Owner of Strategic AlignMint Culinary Services, and a quaint restaurant called CoCo Bistro. Her book, "A Warrior's Sword," released January, 2020, conveys strategies of hope and strength when facing life's challenges.

Walda's revelatory message transcends around the world helping women to stand strong through adversity. As founder of Woman D.A.R.E. To Live, Walda facilitates women of faith to Define, Align, Restore and Expect to live their best life, empowering them to strategically align four key areas: faith, family, finances, and fitness.

Education:
Bachelor's in Ministry Leadership, CFCI Bible Institute
Bachelors in Culinary Arts, International Culinary Schools
Bachelors Purdue University Global, March 2022

Walda and her beloved husband of 25 years, Dr. Keith G. Collins have two sons, Zachary and Keith, Jr.

Author, Speaker, Entrepreneur

Website: www.waldacollins.com
Email: info@waldacollins.com
Facebook: www.facebook.com/walda-collins
Instagram: www.instagram.com/walda_collins

JJ Conway

Stand Up and Say "I can and I will!"
By JJ Conway

When I started school, my teachers told my mom I was slow and I'd never really amount to much. They wrote me off as did most of the world around me. My mom, however, insisted upon a certain second grade teacher, Mrs. Gilmore, who was known to help slow kids succeed. Mrs. Gilmore made it her mission to work with me, and in my last progress report she wrote that my reading and comprehension were on par with my grade level.

I learned from my mom that when the world says you can't, you say, "I can and I will."

The world will always try to put limitations on us, but those limitations don't have to define our future. Most people mean well. They're simply trying to protect us from disappointment, failure, or other harm. They tell you to play small. Some are too disappointed in their own failures to push you to be your best. As Les Brown says, "Other people's opinion of you does not have to become your reality."

I worked hard in school. I was never the smartest kid in the room, but I was always the hardest working. This paid off when I received a full-ride scholarship to the Air Force Academy. Physics wasn't my strongest class, but I thought it was super cool to levitate magnets and design rocket ships. My heart broke when my advisor said I wasn't qualified to declare physics as my major. I pushed back. I had all As and Bs, and a B average was needed. At the time, I was too naive to know how people act when they don't want you around; how they come up with reason after reason why you can't. I kept refuting his reasons until he finally shouted out, "Blacks can't do physics."

"You won't make it. Blacks can't do physics!"

I made up my mind to prove him wrong and declared physics. Though a handful supported me, I found myself rejected by most of my peers and professors. One particular class became so hard, I almost quit. Perhaps that man was right after all! I would go to the professor looking for extra help, and leave more confused than when I went in. After about two months, on a day when all the other professors were gone, he leveled with me. "Look, my job is to get rid of you. If you will stop coming in here, I will stop feeding you the wrong answers."

I stopped going into his office, and in 1997, as president of the Physics and Astronomy Club, I graduated from the Air Force Academy with a bachelor's degree in physics, specializing in space. I earned a full-ride master's degree scholarship and went on to "do physics" for 23 years in the Air Force, serving as the first African American in that role.

A lot of you today were the first person in your family to accomplish something. The first one to graduate from high school. The first one to buy a house. The first doctor, nurse, business owner, teacher.

I'll bet you had a lot of people say, "You can't do it." They told you not to waste your time. You kept going, and you learned for yourself that when the world says you can't, you must decide that, "I can and I will!"

Halfway through my military career, I came home to find my house sold and stuff thrown out. Once the divorce papers were signed, I was a single military mother with over $845,000 of debt. Everyone told me to file bankruptcy. They insisted I'd never overcome this, but I couldn't file bankruptcy! I would lose my security clearance and with it, my job. I needed that job to put food on my table.

Albert Einstein said, "You can't solve today's problems with the same kind of thinking that created them. To make a massive change or overcome a huge obstacle requires a new, creative, way of thinking."

I learned how to hustle in a hurry. I learned how money worked. I started teaching classes on money management and how to invest in real estate without getting into more debt. I now empower and educate others with the same strategies that got me out of my debt.

11 years later, and I am a full-time speaker, trainer, and coach by day and a full-time mom by night.

Life is a series of challenges, and too many of us give up right before our breakthrough. We give up on our dreams, on our calling, on our gifting, on our greatness. We let our vast potential fall by the wayside because so many people tell us we can't. We tell ourselves we aren't good enough, we're not worthy, or that we don't deserve success.

Despite our past successes, the next challenge seems too heavy. We forget how we made it, how the Lord brought us through, and we yield to anxiety and depression.

That's what I did after a car accident left me with post concussive syndrome. Once a scientist who wrote reports for the president, now I couldn't even make Monopoly change with my son. I thought my life was over. At work, I was the office scapegoat and the butt of many jokes. I was spiraling into despair, until a friend reminded me what I told her all those years: "When the world says you can't, you must say, 'I can and I will!' "

I found the right doctors, right supplements, right diet, and today I run an international financial education company. Not perfectly, but perfectly imperfect.

You don't have to be perfect. YOU ARE ENOUGH! I don't know what you're facing right now, but I know that if you can overcome it if you make up your mind, stand up, and say, "I can and I will!"

Bio:

Janine "JJ" Conway, graduated from the Air Force Academy. She was the first African-American to serve as a physicist in the Air Force, where she retired as a Lieutenant Colonel after 23 years. After returning from a military trip to discover her house sold, divorce papers, and over $845,000 debt to her name, JJ had to learn how to hustle in a hurry. Adapting to life as a military single mom, JJ learned how money worked and how to make it work for her quickly, yet ethically. She now teaches others the same personal growth and financial management skills that allowed her to dump debt and begin building wealth. She also mirrors these principles when working with businesses to improve processes, people, and profit.

Take a free class or download JJ's podcast at:
https://www.BuildingWealthTogether.com

Instagram, LinkedIn, YouTube, Facebook, SoundCloud, Twitter, Vimeo: @JJKnowsTheWay

28 Days to Financial Freedom Bootcamp: https://jjclink.com/28

Montrella S. Cowan

Loss, Love, and Life: Overcoming Grief and Fulfilling Your Purpose
By Montrella S. Cowan, MSW, LICSW

'Are you driving?' Prior to the morning of June 20, 2018, I could never have imagined that such a simple inquiry would leave an indelible mark on my heart. However, it did. This was the exact question that the investigative officer asked me repeatedly before delivering the worst news any parent could hear.

One of my biggest lessons in life is that love and grief go hand in hand. However, that fact is a hard pill to swallow. According to Elizabeth Kubler Ross, the five stages of grief are denial, anger, bargaining, depression, and acceptance. These stages are important to keep in mind, as life will "throw a monkey wrench" at us from time to time, especially when we least expect it.

I would never have suspected the words that would come out of the officer's mouth so calmly, "She passed away."

No, not my baby! I screamed and fell to the floor, my face flooded with tears. My co-workers rushed to my office to find out what was going on. My intern picked up the phone and listened to the officer's remaining details of a parent's worst nightmare.

Her name was China. She was 25 years old when she died from Lupus. Her daughter, Sekai, was only five years old. I felt like I was trapped in the Twilight Zone , especially since I was still grieving the loss of my mother who had passed away from heart failure only four months earlier.

Right before the call, I sent an email to my supervisors to let them know that I didn't feel well and was leaving early. I remember feeling strange. In hindsight, it was my motherly intuition telling me that something involving my first-born of two children was wrong.

China and I had made it through so much together. Although I was a virgin when I was raped by her father, she was the most beautiful baby born to me at only 15, and I loved her unconditionally. I was overwhelmed with the responsibility of caring for another, but she was my inspiration to be the best that I could be. It was tough living in poverty, and we had a lot of haters, but I was determined to break the generational curses of abuse, bad relationships, crime, and drug addiction that plagued my family.

You may wonder "How did Montrella beat the odds of such terrible circumstances and losses?" I am glad you asked.

These are four principles that I learned from China and live by that, if followed precisely, will help any woman (or man) crush mediocrity:

1. **Choose to Push Past Your Comfort Zone**
   I can assure you that one of the most petrifying things you will ever do is move past your comfort zone, because it takes courage to do things differently in a world that expects you to follow the norms. Everything starts with a decision. The Almighty God has created you in His own image, and you get to decide how uniquely and fully you want to express him. It is important to honor your values, talents, and passions by choosing what you love.

2. **Have a vision**
   The Bible tells us in Habakkuk 2:2-3,

"…Write the vision, and make it plain upon tables, that he may run that readeth it. For the vision is yet for an appointed time, but at the end, it shall speak, and not lie: though it tarry, wait for it; because it will surely come, it will not tarry."

Perhaps the most crucial step is having a vision. I like to think of it as inputting an address to a GPS. We will not know which direction to travel or when we have arrived without having a destination.

Vision simplifies the journey. Life happens, and people or circumstances may temporarily derail you, but do not give up. The bigger the dream, the steeper the obstacles, but if you do not lose sight of where you are going, these obstacles will not only make you stronger, but light the road on your way to success as well.

3.   **Find Your Tribe**

Have you ever felt frustrated when the people you rely on for support the most desert you? Trust me when I say that this is a familiar feeling.

Whether it be family members, friends, spiritual brothers and sisters, or your romantic partner, rejection will sting like a bee, but we can't take their reasons personally.

Why? Because we each have a different perspective on life.

Once you understand this, you will no longer seek validation in the wrong places. Love them, accept their limitations, and proceed to your dreams. Give up the pity party notion that no one is there for you. Your tribe are those who actively celebrate you and your successes. Do such people still exist in the world? Yes! Your true tribe will not caution you but rather encourage you to go after your next victory. Everything we pray for is already here. God is that good. Keep taking action steps towards your goals and stay in receiving mode to attract good.

4. **Practice an Attitude of Gratitude**

Many of us have cultivated an entitlement mentality- believing privileges are rights. Many parents know how disappointing it is to give their best without being appreciated. Likewise, we can find that we ourselves always ask for more without ever saying thank you. Take a candid look in the mirror. What do you see? Are you an ungrateful child of God? Take a good look around and witness all that God has done for you. It is easy to take blessings for granted. That is, until we lose them. Be grateful, even for things yet to come.

Though my reality has the full alphabet of trauma and tragedy, I'm still standing, helping others, and living my life on purpose. Know that whatever you are going through, you are not alone.

Bio:

Montrella Cowan is a licensed therapist, life coach, transformative speaker, bestselling author, and all-around survivor who inspires everyday people and professionals to step into their greatness by crushing barriers to mental health and wellness through motivational speaking, life coaching, and therapy.

A firm believer in the mantra #TruthOverTrauma, Montrella is no stranger to trauma. Montrella hails from the inner city projects of Brooklyn, New York where she was raised by a crack-addicted mother, sexually abused as a teenager, and surrounded by a plethora of generational woes including incarceration, welfare dependency, and extreme poverty.

The taxing nature of her past, including being raped at 14, giving birth at 15, and then losing that daughter to Lupus at the age of 25, has given Montrella an exceptional ear for listening, understanding and working with clients. She founded Affinity Health Affairs.

If you're ready to smash the past and co-create your future, Montrella can show you how. Visit her at Affinity411.com.

Chriscilia Lyles Cox

Seriously Though, Come Get Your____
By Chriscilia Lyles Cox

Have you ever become so angry or upset that you reached a place that was not your character? Did you ask yourself how you got there in the first place? It is possible, and I know I'm not the only one who has had this experience.

Dear God, I want to thank you for everything thus far in my life. Today is yet another day I have never seen before. If something happens to me, please let my baby live and me die. She deserves to live life better than me and enjoy all possibilities. At this time, I would like to truly forgive anyone who has wronged me in your sight as you have forgiven me. I know I haven't done everything you have asked, but don't let my child pay for my mistakes. She will make many mistakes herself. She shouldn't pay twice. God, let her grow up to be an exceptional human being and to get it right where I didn't. Have someone share my life, accomplishments, differences I made on this side of heaven with her. These things I ask in thy name. Amen.

After this prayer, I hugged my belly and felt an unexplainable peace like I'd never felt before. I put on my military maternity uniform, glanced in the mirror, and conducted my last-minute hygiene. Why was I compelled to say such a prayer before leaving my house? Did I know something was about to happen? Was something about to happen to my daughter? No. All I knew was I had to get this off my chest. The rest of the day's events would make me think twice about allowing others to determine my fate.

Later that day, I went into preeclampsia, with a blood pressure reading of 220 over 114. My daughter's monitor reading was ten. She was stable, and her heart rate was average. However, tons of IV bags of hydralazine were necessary to stabilize me. When I came to, I found myself in the hospital connected to all types of monitors with tubes up my veins. I even had an oxygen tank and compression socks. I was still able to have my baby vaginally.

After giving birth, I felt embarrassed, defeated, and at my lowest. Drugs were administered to me until I was in a hallucinogenic state. I was so hallucinogenic that I saw the Jolly Green Giant rowing across the floor of my room. It scared me so much, I hit the panic button. My healthcare team took me off hydralazine and started my homecare drug regimen. It was days before I could breastfeed or hold my newborn, which added doubt to my recovery. I was confident that I couldn't care for my child effectively. After that, I fell into a more profound depressive state.

One morning, I got up around two A.M. I started cleaning the room and combed my hair. I must have scared the nurse as she was expecting me to still be in my hospital bed looking at the ceiling. Then, after I hadn't spoken for days, I said " Good morning." I remembered saying my prayers the night before. I woke up refreshed and finally found my inner strength. That strength continued until I recovered and went home.

Growing up in a southeastern, rural area was challenging, but helped many- like myself- build character, tenacity, courage, respect, grit, and heart. We learn never to settle for anything but the best. However, some of those lessons were more realistic to where we lived versus the world outside our area. Classes are from testimonies about living, but they revolved around having respect. Our local expectation outside was a standard to reach. In reality, I found this wasn't the case. It's even more disappointing for individuals who should understand and appreciate these same standards, for our environments were very similar.

Every chapter of my life has had excitement, adventure, the continuance of striving to create a better version of myself, and hitting personal milestones. My physics professor told me to lower my military expectations because it was hard for African Americans to receive opportunities. I cringed at this statement. At the time, I was attending a historically black university. That professor was stumped when I graduated with my commission as a medical service corps officer and class valedictorian. This was the beginning of multiple achievements in my military career. Though trouble-free, generous, and empowered with the confidence that I could do anything, my destiny was distant.

Toward the end of my career, I finally accepted that I would not advance to the next rank.

Although I had accepted this, I planned to be great outside the organization. I started strategically planning and making necessary connections. However, my transition into my exciting, new norm was greeted by backstabbing, harassment, accusations, and worse. Most of these situations led to episodes of depression, anxiety, and other self-doubts.

The truth is that the prayer I mentioned at the beginning of this chapter was from the day I was supposed to have died. I vaguely remember how my leadership reacted when I was admitted into the hospital. While being pregnant, they knew they ultimately stressed me out through countless unnecessary and vile episodes. A few years ago, it was revealed to me that my administration hoped that I made it through that night. During this time, my leadership continued to harass me because I was still in the hospital. After I retired; my administration continued to harass me. I learned that evil has no color and not to let others determine my fate.

Every situation or obstacle wants you to get sucked in and make "it" your reality. Actually, "it" belongs elsewhere or to someone other than you. When you get to this space, say to yourself, "Seriously though, come get your_____." Remember, the blank is applicable towards your situation.

Bio:

Chriscilia Lyles Cox is a unique brand strategist known for using her gift of management, team building, and strategic thinking to help people solve problems cost-effectively using communication and innovation. After retiring from the military, she found SUMA Consulting LLC, an environmental management and sustainability firm where she helps businesses, organizations, and families.

"As a military veteran, I have been responsible for growing client bases, driving environmental and sustainability goal setting, and leading budgets and cost savings for the Department of Defense. I am happy that I can still live out my dream and make a difference."

Chriscilia lives in Georgia with her husband and daughter. Her civic involvements include various volunteer, leadership and national board roles.

For more information on SUMA, visit www.sumaconsulting.org. You can also follow her on

Facebook:	@sumaconsultingllc.
Instagram:	sumaconsulting
LinkedIn:	chriscilia-cox-ma-14b8a0108

61

Min. Nakita Davis

Positioned to WIN!
By Min. Nakita Davis

I am Woman, hear me roar! This is a good time to be a woman and an even greater time to be you!

You are a woman with a sound mind, walking in purpose, soaring in your God-given talents, bridging the gap between hopelessness, and delivering on what is possible.

God is good.

The question quickly becomes: how do you level-up on this unique time created just for you? How do you tap into your God-given Power and Unleash the Greatness inside of You to Win and WIN BIG?

Queen, It's Time to Play Your Royal Position.

I present to you, the Q.U.E.E.N. concept that I personally use to crush mediocrity, silence the inner critic, and live a life of purpose and grace.

Pillar #1

- QUIT Making Excuses!

Queen, this is pivotal to achieving the success, purpose, and authority given to you before you were even in your mother's womb.

You must take full inventory of the people, places, things, negative self-talk, and self-limiting beliefs that have kept you stuck, stagnant, and stale.

I had to do the same.

I had to remove the excuse of comfortability.

I was that little girl from the hood who grew up surrounded by drugs, violence, prostitution, alcoholism, food stamps, and impoverished mindsets.

Although my God-fearing parents did their best to provide, we still struggled financially.

How many know that it's not about where you start but where you finish?

Glory to God, what we lacked in money, my parents overcompensated with love. Despite the sounds of gunshots lulling me to sleep, I always knew that something greater was on the way.

I did well in school and landed a 'good paying job.'

After all, I was taught to go to school, work, and raise a family along the way.

But somewhere along that journey, God spoke greater into my life.

In order to truly CRUSH mediocrity and walk into my land of milk and honey, I had to get comfortable with being uncomfortable.

Pillar #2

- Understand Your Assignment

Sis, this life is not for the faint of heart. To achieve greatness, you must understand the weight of your calling.

During this process, I had to ask myself tough questions to propel forward.

- Who are you called to serve and why?

- What Impact are you called to make and how?

- Why is this your time to do the very thing you were put on this earth to do?

- What is the weight of saying 'yes' to your calling, and what will happen if you say no?

Your questions may look slightly different, but all roads should lead to the fulfillment of your destiny.

When you understand the weight of your calling, you will begin to move, walk, and talk in a deliberate manner that aligns you with your purpose.

Queen, you have no time to lose.

Pillar #3

- Enlist Your Supporting Cast

Simply put, your tribe matters!

Collaborate with nine millionaires and you will be the tenth.

Lollygag with nine other people who make excuses, and you will be the tenth too.

Enlisting your supporting cast is your Call to Action. It separates the wheat from the chaff.

Can I keep it real, Queen?

In this precise moment, you are not reading this by mistake or chance.

There are people who no longer serve your vision, mission, or calling over your life. This includes friends, family, and associates too.

Your Land of Milk and Honey awaits your keen wisdom and discernment in this hour.

Keeping the right people in your corner is no longer a luxury but a necessity to accomplishing your purpose!

Choose wisely.

Pillar #4

- Establish Your Winning Team

Set clear expectations and teach people how to support you is imperative to crushing mediocrity.

I had to strategically align myself with like-hearted Queens who wanted to see me WIN.

Collaboration over competition.

Instead of looking for people who were never designed to support me, I fixed my focus on supporters of the vision.

Effectively communicating how my tribe can help me and how I can serve them has led to countless wins for my entire team. #winningisahabit

The same can happen for You!

Pillar #5

- NOW

When you have a fire in the pit of your belly, You Must Let it OUT!

Sadly, Queen, many will leave this Earth with their full potential uncapped.

Queen, do not let that be you!

Your NOW is NOW!

Fast-Forward

When I decided to trust God at His word, He showed up and showed out.

#watchGodwork

On December 30th, 2019, I decided to walk away from my corporate job of nearly 15 years to pursue my full-time business: Jesus, Coffee, and Prayer Christian Publishing House LLC.

Operating in obedience to God, faith, love, and a whole lot of 'sweat equity,' I went from earning $2,000 a month in my business to clearing over $30,000 dollars monthly within a year.

Yassss God!

He added His SUPER to my natural and exponentially grew my YES over a few things to a six figure, thriving business during the pandemic.#WontHeDoIt

My best-selling publishing company has expanded to help women worldwide gain visibility, credibility, and authority in their speaking, writing, and Girlboss business. Up next-Television.

The Women Win NETWORK (television network) will enter the homes of millions spring of 2021!

Nobody but God!

I share not to brag on me but to boast in God!

If you want to know my 'secret sauce' to crushing mediocrity and bossing up like never-before,

I would love to introduce you to a man named Jesus.

Queen, I am not here to preach to you nor sway you.

But I am here to encourage you to walk into your GREATER!

Walk away knowing that you are loved and worthy of winning.

You are ONE YES away from Crushing Mediocrity, Crashing Ceilings, and Breaking Generational Curses.

Queen, It's Time to Play Your Royal Position!

Bio:

Min. Nakita Davis is the Proud CEO & Founder of Jesus, Coffee, and Prayer Christian Publishing House LLC. The #1 Christian Publishing House in the Land. Her team helps Women of Faith birth their Best-Selling/International Best-Selling books fast! Known as the Atlanta Book Hit-Maker, her firm helps Women to gain the visibility, credibility, and authority their speaker, author, girlboss business deserves by providing global virtual stages, marketing, media, and PR. The media maven now adds The Women WIN NETWORK~ a television network produced by Women for Women Who WIN!

Through ROKU, Amazon Fire TV & more, her network will reach nearly 100 Million homes nationally and globally. Min. Davis is married to her childhood sweetheart and lives with their 2 beautiful children in Atlanta, GA. Jesus is the Source of her Strength.

Stay Connected:
Facebook & Instagram: @jesuscoffeeandprayer
Clubhouse   @minnakitadavis
Website: www.jesuscoffeeandprayer.com
Let's Work Together, email all inquiries:
info@jesuscoffeeandprayer.com

Monique Denton-Davis

You Don't Know How Good You Are, I Had Enough
By Monique Denton-Davis

"You don't know how good you are." I'd heard this three times in my professional career, and by the third time, I had enough!

I will never forget something that happened over 15 years ago, when I was grieving the loss of my grandfather. I was sitting at work with my Executive VP, a gray haired, middle- aged white man from Texas.

It was my performance review time. As we went through the different categories; Communication, Collaboration, Problem- solving, etc., I found myself listening but not listening. I thought about how much I missed my grandfather and how I wanted this meeting to end. I have always considered myself to be a high performer. I was not surprised that I scored above average in each category. However, the longer I sat in the meeting, the more discontent I became as I felt that the VP showed no empathy for my loss. I considered it torture and wanted it to end. At that time, I was a Human Resources Manager with an HR team of one, responsible for all New York locations with about 300 employees. The remainder of the team was based out of our corporate headquarters in Connecticut . Not only was I the only one in New York , I was the only person of color on our entire team.

Finally, my performance review came to an end. I was relieved. My VP said that based on my high rating, I was eligible for the maximum increase of a "whopping" four percent ! I said ok. Then he asked if I had any comments, questions, or anything I'd like to add. I thought of something cliche, and said , "It's a pleasure working for the company." Then he looked at me, paused, and said , "You know, Monique, you don't know how good you are!" "Wait a minute," I said to myself, "Did this man just say what I think he said?" I was at full attention then. My sadness turned to anger, and I immediately began to have a real sister girl conversation in my mind, complete with questions and answers. I saw my head turning to check and see if there was anyone else in the room. However, I quickly composed myself, and although I had that brief moment of disbelief, my posture, body language and facial expression remained completely unchanged.

You see, it's not that I didn't know how good I was because I certainly did. I, like most women, especially women of color, was taught to be seen and not heard. I was taught not to talk over, or dominate conversations at work. I was taught not to be a "Miss Know- it- All," even if I was the expert. I was taught to be respectable in a passive, assertive type of way and, of course, the number one deal breaker, never allow myself to be perceived as the stereotypical angry and aggressive black woman.

So I, like most women during that time, was afraid to be authentic. Afraid to be who I truly was. Afraid to show too much intelligence. . Afraid to talk over or to say something that would make my superiors look at me with discontent. You see, this was long before the "Me Too" movement. This was at a time when corporate America did not acknowledge strong women leaders or women leadership, especially women of color.

I knew that I was not the only one. Research clearly shows that women are less likely to speak up in meetings, negotiate salaries, negotiate job offers, or negotiate promotions. And why? Oftentimes it's because we felt that it was inappropriate and not our place. We were afraid of losing our jobs if we spoke up or outshined our male counterparts. It has taken us years of cognitive dissonance, constantly fighting our own thoughts, beliefs, and sometimes even culture- the way we were raised, what our parents and aunties and uncles taught us- to voice what we've always internalized: that we, as women, deserve more. We deserve equality and the chance to be our authentic, true selves both inside and outside of the workplace.

In early 2019, a study conducted by Korn Ferry indicated the percentage of women among the top 1,000 highest-grossing companies in C-suite positions was at 25 percent , slightly up from 23 percent in 2018. Of that 25 percent , only 6 percent% were actually CEOs.

I digressed from my performance review. I left out explaining what the Executive VP said to me, "You don't know how good you are." Something inside of me sparked. All of a sudden, I no longer cared about values. I no longer cared about being inappropriate. I was no longer fearful of disrespect. I no longer feared losing my job or sounding like the stereotypical angry black women. I simply stated, as calmly as I could, "Well if you know how good I am, why doesn't my salary reflect my work?" My VP looked at me, somewhat in disbelief but not with anger or discontent. He paused, sighed, hesitated and then said, "You know Monique, you're right. I'm not going to give you a 4 percent increase. I'm going to add an additional $10,000 annually to your salary.." At that moment, I made a vow to myself that I would never again be afraid to stand in my truth both inside and outside of the workplace.

How do you get to being fearless and living in your truth? There's levels to this. My mantra is "no woman left behind." As a Certified Life Transformation Coach, I am dedicated to helping aspiring entrepreneurs, business professionals, and women looking to define their life's vision and purpose. You know you're a leader. Learn how to step outside of the box, get unstuck, and walk in your truth. Visit me at www.embraceyourcake.com

Bio:

Monique Denton-Davis is a sought- after motivational speaker, certified life transformation coach, and author of several books, including her recent Indie Author Legacy award nominated anthology, *Unapologetically Winning*! Monique is the Founder & CEO of Embrace Your CAKE, LLC, Life Coaching. Focusing on Confidence, Attitude, Kindness and Excellence.

For over 20+ years, Monique has held numerous leadership positions in the human resources field, including human resources director, training and recruitment director, executive level recruiter, and corporate trainer. She is certified in Human Resource Management, Diversity and Inclusion and Nonviolent Crisis Intervention. She holds a degree in Business Administration. She utilizes all of her experiences when working with clients, and strategizes not only their personal lives but their careers as well. She works collaboratively with clients to identify career goals, explore options, overcome obstacles, and set goals with accountability. She believes that self-awareness and empowerment allows women to break through barriers and uncover their true potential.

Social Media: @embraceyourcake
Website: embraceyourcake.com
Email: monique@embraceyourcake

Cynthia A. Gipson Lee

My Healing After the Healing
By Cynthia A. Gipson Lee

I was in pain 24 hours a day; excruciating physical pain. Throbbing, aching, shooting pain in my wrists, neck, shoulders, hips, knees, and more. After being diagnosed with fibromyalgia, my life took on a completely new look. A look that I could not have planned for or imagined. Yet, over the course of two years, my faith grew, my support increased, and my pain completely healed. God gave me a testimony.

However, this story isn't about that healing.

It's about my healing *after* the healing.

Don't get me wrong, that journey was incredible. I suffered from a condition said to be incurable. Medicine could only help manage the pain so that I could possibly have a better quality of life. God reached down, touched me, and healed me. Hallelujah!

After the physical healing, God gave me the vision to share my story with a book. I hesitated. What had I done with my healing? Over a decade had passed since my fibromyalgia pain ended. Yet, I felt like I wasn't living my life to the fullest. I felt I should be doing more than surviving. I should be thriving with my restored health.

After that, I took a critical look at myself and made a list of areas in my life that needed to change. There were a lot! Well, how should I fix them? I prayed and asked God to show me.

God's answer? "I've already shown you!"

Months back, I attended a church event, where a beloved church mother shared a family tradition. Before evening prayers with her kids, each of them recited a scripture. What an amazing idea! I was inspired to curate a personal list of scriptures I started to memorize for myself.

When God woke me up from my flashback, I read those scriptures, which were hanging above my desk. Each of my memorized verses matched an issue in my life that needed a makeover. Everything started to click.

I gave God a high-five for the awesome assist, and my planning superpower started to kick in. "Thanks, God. I've got it from here." I created an outline for the book, built an action plan for a program, and even created goals around my trouble areas. Things began coming together.

Suddenly, dates started slipping. I started to miss goals and become discouraged. I wasn't making headway. Weeks, months, even years went by, and I didn't see any progress.

I went back to God and asked, "What's wrong? You helped me identify the areas, I came up with plans, but they're not working. Now what?"

Just as I sought God for healing from fibromyalgia, I realized I needed to involve God in this new healing as well. Letting go of material things. Getting a better hold of my schedule. Living a healthy lifestyle. I couldn't just resolve these areas alone.

I needed to involve God in all of my mess.

That's what was missing. My healing was bigger than me. It also wasn't only for me.

You may have your own "Now what?" situation. Like me, you may feel like you keep adding things to your "unfinished" list. Abandoned goals. Unhealthy life habits. You may feel like you're letting yourself and God down.

Now what? What should you do differently? How do you move forward? I believe we're meant to do more than live unfinished. Through the "cynergy" of God + You + Me, we can create change.

These are the three steps God gave me to create Cynergy in my life:

- Get honest with myself
- Get humble before God
- Get help from others

GET HONEST
What's something that's holding you back? List a few areas where you feel stuck. Don't get overwhelmed if it seems like a lot. Ask God to help you know where to start.

GET HUMBLE
Go before God and acknowledge you cannot do this alone. Pray. Study. Seek God's will for your life in these areas. Find a focus scripture to ground you. Memorize it. Write it in your own words. Lean on God and God's Word for strength.

GET HELP
Find others to help keep you accountable for your progress. Be sure this includes those who will pray with and for you. Develop an action plan towards your goal, and enlist professionals where needed. Encouragement and education are important.

Get ready, because God will show up.

The first scripture I focused on was Joshua 1:8, which I subtitled, "God as My Priority." My area of improvement was to study God's Word, so I set aside time to read one verse in Psalm 119 each day. After a few days, I fizzled out. Even though it seemed as if I failed, God had a different plan.

During this time, God gave me the idea for Will You 52? (WY52). Weekly praise, prayer, and thanks for people who have blessed me. I put my Cynergy project on hold as I started to follow God's breadcrumbs. When I looked at where I was after my year long WY52 journey, God astounded me yet again. I had grown closer to God through intercessory prayers and Bible study as I lived out WY52. I made God a priority. God, you did it again!

It's been an amazing experience to receive gifts from God through each of my scriptures. I continue to enjoy each one even through my growing pains. They are examples, wrapped in models, sitting next to lessons. I realized it wasn't all about my planning. We may not follow the exact path that we prescribe for our healing, and that's ok. God's ways aren't like ours. It's about trust. I needed to give God my full trust.

We should allow for these intentional interruptions, divine detours, and miracle moments. These "surprises" are where the awesomeness of God resides. Make time with God and for God to receive our healing from God. By being honest with yourself, leaning on God, and working with others, your healing will come.

Bio:
"Uniquely created and designed to be a blessing to others; using what God has gifted me with and the experiences God has brought me through."

This is Cynthia A. Gipson Lee's mission and assignment from God.

The journey through her life's story has prepared her to creatively share God's goodness with others. Technology, training, and testimony have been major components of Cynthia's life. From her childhood pop-up greeting card store to a long career as a Software Engineer. Entrepreneurship is where she's brought the three together.

Founder of Will You 52? (a ministry rooted in intercessory prayer), her Cynergy Workout is a natural next step. Birthed from Cynthia's testimony of healing, the "cynergy" of God + You + Me has been impactful. Join her as she aspires towards living her best for God.

Learn more about Cynthia and how you can partner with her at:
- cynthiagipsonlee.com
- cynergyworkout.com
- willyou52.com

Mijiza A. Green

Brooklyn Made Me, But Could Not Break Me

By Mijiza A. Green

Brooklyn! The home of Biggie and Jay Z. The place that I grew up, and the place that almost broke me. The place I experienced so many traumatizing events in my life. A place where I can still hear in the back of my head the words of people saying, "Do not worry, Mijiza. Everything is going to be okay." Words I heard from family members as I gave birth to my first child at the age of 13. Words I heard from the doctor right before he performed the C-section that scarred me for life. Words I heard from friends as they left for college, and I stayed behind. From close friends the first time I experienced domestic violence. From those who witnessed the murder of my son's father. From the psychiatrist who admitted me into the hospital. All this by the age of 17. By that point, those words meant nothing to me. Life was not okay and would never be in my mind. Brooklyn, the place I thought I loved, was killing me softly. I started to think this was all life had to offer so I might as well just accept it.

But I couldn't! I could not accept that this was my life. That all I had been through had no purpose. That all the dreams and ideas in my head were not real. A single, teen mother. That was it. I was more than that. I wanted more, and I had to figure it out. Brooklyn seemed to only bear the fruit of high school dropouts, teen pregnancy, death, domestic violence, and trauma. This was all I saw, all I knew, but I was not going to be like everyone else. I wanted more, not just for me, but for my son. I could not let him grow up in the place that almost took my life. I packed my bags, woke my son, and we took a car and never looked back. We drove straight to Maryland in the middle of the night. This was it. There was no turning back. I showed up at my sister's doorstep, and she welcomed me in without a clue what I was doing there. I told her I needed a break. I wanted to start a new life for my son, and she helped make it happen. Little did she know, I found myself once again in a violent relationship which I hid from my family. Many of my friends knew about it and even witnessed some of the brutality, but there was nothing they could do because they too were experiencing similar trauma. Somehow, this became the norm. It became accepted that being beat was just part of the relationship and a way of expressing love. That was not the kind of love I was looking for, and it was not going to be my norm.

As I look back, I am proud of myself for making such a drastic decision at the age of 21. God saved my life. If I had done what was easy and stayed in Brooklyn continuing to allow people to treat me like trash, life would have become even harder. I decided to do what was hard- leave and start fresh when everyone counted me out and insisted I would be back. They said I would not make it, but I did. God had a different plan. I was never mediocre. The fight was always inside me. The desire to be great, to share my story, and talents with the world was already there. I simply had to take a step out of faith, and follow my heart, which I did. I realized that rejection, fear, and shame were my three biggest demons. I always felt like others would not hear me or that I was not good enough to be a motivational speaker. Eventually, I realized that people were not rejecting me, they were rejecting themselves. They were not ready to face their truth. I was doing what I was called to do: holding people accountable for their actions and words. I created a space to be a mirror to other women. Many of them did not want to see the truth, lies, and hurt. Fear was the recognition that I was growing in areas of my life I didn't even know existed. Fear was the fight inside of me that would not settle for an average life. I wanted what God had promised: a life of abundance. I understand now that if I was not afraid then I was not growing, so I embraced fear when it came, and I said "Thank you, Lord." Shame allowed me to surrender to God and accept that I no longer had to blame myself. I had to forgive others for hurting me and myself for carrying the baggage around for so long. When I embraced this, I realized I crushed mediocrity. Life did not change- I did. When I changed my mindset, I changed my life. When I changed my perceptions of life, I changed my circumstances. I began to tell my story to impact and inspire others to do the same. I give them hope that it is possible, because this woman from Brooklyn changed the game. Today, you can make the same decision to crush mediocrity by getting mentally motivated with me at the Wellness Purse. Today, decide to put yourself first, to be the best version of yourself, and change the game. You do not have to be like everybody else. You are wonderfully and uniquely made, and it's time to show the world. So, what are you waiting for? Go to www.thewellnesspurse.com and start the process of crushing it!

Bio:

Mijiza Green is the owner of The Wellness Purse, where she works as a life strategist that mentally motivates youth and women by building character, confidence, and courage through her S.E.L.F techniques. Stop, Evaluate, Listen and Forgive in order to better manage your life and obtain positive mental health. She is also alongside her husband, the creator of youth programs such Treasured Jewels Mentor Program, Young Men Empowered and GRACE Empowerment that has Inspired, Educated, and Impacted the lives of youth in Maryland and surrounding areas.

Mijiza is an impactful speaker, mentor, and author of the children's book ,"Pretty to be Dark-Skinned". If you are ready to set goals, pursue your dreams, and get mentally motivated with Mijiza, she can be reached at www.thewellnesspurse.com @justmimi1979 on IG or Mijiza Green on Facebook

Regina C. Hall

Come Out, Come Out, Wherever You Are!
By Regina C. Hall

When I was growing up, we played a game called "Hide and Seek." I loved the fun and the excitement hiding and hoping that no one would find me brought. I remained silent, my body tight to make sure that I was not found. I hoped that my giggles would not be heard. My heart pounded and waited to hear the seeker call, "Come out, come out, wherever you are!" Finally, I would be found and tagged, and the seeker and I would burst into laughter. What a game! I believe that game resembled the way I had lived most of my life. It was somewhat apparent to me but not as clear as it is now. I lived life hidden but desperately needing to be found if I was to achieve my life's goals.

Acclaimed author and life coach John C. Maxwell stated, "The greatest gap in life is the one between knowing and doing." We may know what to do, but not do it. Not knowing doesn't mean that I did not accomplish great things in life. I have had some remarkable opportunities, and I believe that seizing them contributed to the person I am today. However, I sensed that I was not fulfilling my purpose and would eventually feel stuck, disillusioned, and frustrated.

When I was a little girl around about five years old, I recall seeing a vision of what appeared to be a large group in an auditorium. I was an international speaker. I could not visualize the faces of the individuals, but I felt their presence. It was a young adult version of myself. I could not see myself, but I sensed myself. Throughout the years, I continued seeing glimpses of that vision. As quickly as I saw them, they disappeared. I wondered to myself, "Is that what I am called to do? Speak?" Was I called to preach? I knew that God had purposed it in my heart.

My first experience going to church was one of the most beautiful events I have ever experienced. I was between about five and seven years of age. I remember wearing a pretty dress, hat, and black patent leather shoes with short, white, ruffled socks. I felt pretty, and I was excited about where my dad was taking us. My mom was asleep on the sofa, and I tried to wake her, but I could not, so we left. When I walked into the church, I saw so many people all dressed up. I saw beautiful, colorful windows that I would later learn were called "stained glass." The church had a high ceiling, or at least it appeared that way to me. The choir was seated directly behind the pastor. I had never heard a choir sing before. They sounded angelic. They were singing about Jesus. As they sang, I saw a light shine through the window. I was so drawn to this light that I felt it was more than just the sun. I experienced a sense of peace, and joy filled my heart.

When the service was over, I could not wait to get home to my mom. She was awake, and I told her all about the singing and how they talked about Jesus. I did not want the feeling to end. I told my parents that I wanted to go to church from then on, and I started attending the neighborhood church.

I became very active in my church. One would have thought my calling was solidified and understood, but this was not the case. I hid from my calling due to anger, fear, rejection, and sadness.

A few years ago, I wrote a book called *Mommy, I Need You!* The purpose of the book was to share my story of the sexual abuse I suffered at the hands of a next-door neighbor, and to encourage women to get involved in the lives of other women who are broken and hurt from traumatic experiences. The more women are healed, the more our daughters will live healthy lives. Sexual abuse can stifle a victim and permeate throughout her life. The sexual abuse, along with other circumstances of my life, some my own doing, impacted my ability to believe in myself.

My life started to change after I married my first husband. I felt safe with him, and although we were not perfect, I was able to exhale. I had prayed to God that if he allowed me to marry, I would read His word and build a better relationship with Him. I kept my word. I studied God's Word daily while my husband was at work. I also started a master's program in Pastoral Counseling. I was deep into the word of God, so much so that when my husband came home, he found me asleep, surrounded by books.

The Bible says in James 4:8, "Come near to God and he will come near to you." I drew near to God by studying His Word, attending Church, and participating in Bible studies started my journey of crushing mediocrity. However, if anyone had told me that in drawing near to God, I would endure an extreme, mental makeover, I would have told them, "Thanks, but I'm good." The healing process forced me to confront the thoughts and images that I had about myself. My self-esteem was at my feet.

I was fighting for my mind like fighting for my last breath. I was in the valley of despair, sadness, suicidal thoughts, rejection, abandonment, and unforgiveness, but the Bible was my source. I learned three valuable lessons in the valley. One, I had to let go of the past because God was doing a new thing in me. The pains and hurts of the past could no longer define me. God was pruning me. Two, I had to forgive my abuser and those who had failed to protect me. I learned that forgiveness is about me, not the perpetrators. Finally, I learned that that valley was intended for me to pass through, not for me to remain in. The rewards were on the other side. I was set free from the bondage and chains of my yesterdays. Although I experienced the loss of my father and a divorce shortly after, God brought me through. I now live a life of exploring God, being of sober mind, and letting go of the past.

Come out, come out, wherever you are! You're it!

Bio:
Regina Hall is the president of Enlighten Heart Services LLC, an International Transformational Speaker and Trainer. Regina speaks life to women struggling in their lives, careers, and spiritual journeys to move from pain to purpose. She is the author of "Mommy, I Need You!" where she shares her story of the trauma she suffered at the hands of a next-door neighbor to inspire, uplift, and educate on the importance of healing.

Regina's passion for empowering is echoed in the testimonials of her Masterminds, training, and coaching. She is a certified John Maxwell member, Les Brown motivational speaker, licensed professional counselor (LPC), and an ordained minister.

When Regina is not speaking, she loves spending time with her family, her dog Chloe, and studying the Word of God. Regina resides with her loving husband of 14 years. They have one amazing daughter Amanda.

Marlice Harris-Simon

Girl, That Veil Ain't Yours
By Marlice Harris-Simon

Let the light out.

Your light is beautiful; a unique glow that is critical to the world. The light within you is a piece to a greater 'light puzzle.'

In the light, things are clearer – joy, love, confidence, our purpose. The warrior in us stands tall, and others can see their way through our glow.

Veiled in darkness, purpose is non-existent. Doubt, fear, hopelessness, and insecurity are amplified. In this state, we hear only the noise. We feel trapped and hurt, and sometimes we hurt other people.

We see people who are living with their light at full wattage. It is joyful and energizing to be in their presence. They see only possibilities and inspire us to live our best life.

We also see people who are living veiled! They feel unhappy, directionless, and plagued by bad choices in life, or constantly throw 'shade' at everything and everyone. They live mainly in Negativity ville.

It may be you feeling trapped and directionless. That was me and on some days still is. Even though I have spent years stripping off the layers through fitness and meditation and teaching others how to do the same, there are still days when I can't see or be the light. Perfection is not a human trademark. We aren't built to shine all day, every day. Life will knock us down unexpectedly. In these situations, we can retreat to what we know— a place veiled in hurt, fear, doubt, and even downright anger. The beautiful part is we have the choice to lean into that moment and recognize that shining our lights is more rewarding than staying in darkness. We can use unexpected situations to make us stronger and shine our light brighter to walk in purpose and love.

Living veiled

I am the "commander in chief" of veil- wearing. When this book is published, I will be 45 years old, and I must say, your girl looks good 😊. I spent half my life hiding myself in the lies of others. Girl, I layered them on! Veil #1 – "you will never be good enough; you came from a family that has nothing." Veil #2 – "you are used up; you can't and will never be a good partner to anyone." Veil #3 – "you cannot be anything beyond your horrible past of sexual wildness, lying, and cheating; no one will listen to anything you have to say."

Veil # 3 was my postal code for most of my life. I believed that veil to my core. Even writing now, I feel like hiding under a table. Those words still pierce my sides deeply.

As a young, shining light, eloquent speaker, and community activist, I showed a "lot of promise" to be a great leader. Somewhere on the path to being the "promising one," I found myself pregnant at 19. Bewildered and gripped with the fear of disappointing others, I did what I thought best and got an abortion, which of course did not remain a secret in such a small town.

You see, 'promising,' young, bright girls like me weren't supposed to have sex before marriage, get pregnant, and have abortions. How shameful! My parents and siblings were rock stars; they held me together, but it didn't matter. I believed everything other people said about me. The leaders I trusted said I was "a bad example for girls, " that I had "wrecked my chances of anyone ever seeing me as anything." I thought they must be true, right? If my leaders are telling me, they must be true. The first piece of my veil was secured— 'shame' and 'not good enough.' In that new state of darkness, I retaliated. I set out to prove them right. I hurt many people with my words and actions. I wanted everyone to feel how I felt.— Oh, "bad example? " Watch me. I destroyed whatever came into my path and acted like I didn't care. I lived the stories others told about me because I was too afraid to tell my own truth. I didn't know how to remove the veil of lies I had so willingly put on. Wallowing in that darkness, I believed what others said about me. When we are too afraid to remove our veils and let our light shine through by telling our stories, others tell them for us.

What followed was several years of searching in the dark. Woman, who are you? I made myself sick and created a toxic environment by clutching to those veils. I saw only a path of destruction and shame. Several bouts of depression and suicide attempts brought me full circle. In a final moment of despair , I saw my daughter's face. I asked myself, " Is this the legacy you want her and other women to inherit? Because you chose to hold onto lies and mistakes from 26 years ago?" That was my pivotal moment. I wrote on a piece of paper, "THIS IS NOT YOUR VEIL NOR YOUR LEGACY."

We have experiences for a reason. They shape our lives, our stories, and bring out the best in us; they are part of our becoming. Our pasts are woven into every fiber of our beings, but we don't have to be trapped by them . The choice? Use your experience to fuel your light, not cover it up. Remove the darn veil, it ain't yours. Step unapologetically in your light.

She removed the veils, no longer living according to society's expectations. She is NON-NEGOTIABLE. She gently put down the things that no longer served her, and let her light shine.

Unapologetically FREE, the Almighty shines through her. Don't mourn for the 'her' you once knew. She is no more courageous than you. She made a choice to let go and step boldly into purpose.

Be inspired and courageous. Push past limitations.

BE UNAPOLOGETICALLY YOU. THAT VEIL AIN'T YOURS. LET YOUR LIGHT SHINE!

Bio:

Marlice Harris-Simon is the founder of TheMarliceTrain, a health and wellness coaching hub that focuses on the holistic health and well being of women through fitness, nutrition, and spirituality. She has dedicated her life to empowering women and young girls to be leaders and stand tall in their purpose with authenticity. Marlice equips women with the tools they need to love themselves from the inside out and embrace the body they are in to live a balanced, healthy, lifestyle.

Harris-Simon lives in Ontario, Canada but is originally from Guyana, South America. She has represented her home country at many international fora advocating for the rights of girls and women. Marlice believes that women hold the absolute power within to effect change and shake up the status quo, especially if they are healthy, well and empowered and given the space for their voices to be heard.

Instagram and Facebook: @themarlicetrain

Carmen M. Herrera

What I Had to Offer was Me!
By Carmen M. Herrera

I looked around the room and thought, "I made it! Girl, you are exactly where you planned to be, a room filled with success and money." Despite that, I couldn't rid myself of the annoyance of being eyeballed by the men who couldn't accept I was there. I spent years busting my ass to propel to the top in a white male-dominated industry. None of their expressions read what they should have. Every time I made my confident, bold entrance, I felt their irritation. They struggled to hold their composure. They just couldn't get it, "How did she get here?" Many times, I found my carefully selected classy, professional business attire mentally peeled from my body. Blind to how hard I worked to get to where I was, they only saw the physical attributes. I was determined to overcome this harassment and abuse because I understood these were distractions from a bigger purpose. Many men I worked with could never get past the skirt.

Vice President of a Fortune 500 company, I was forced to do things for myself unlike male VP's, I didn't want to be labeled the "pushy bitch!" I didn't even get respect from female staff who also couldn't believe I was there. Our office had a hundred Financial Advisors, I was the only Advisor of color. On the surface it appeared this disparity wasn't racial, it was there. The Advisors I worked with were decent people, they just struggled with my invasion into their world. I was blessed to have a strong, supportive family background. Being the only girl helped me succeed in a male-dominated industry. It equipped me to persevere and get these men to the realization that all of my brothers had eventually reached: "She's a girl!" Yes, I was a woman and good at what I did.

Please don't mistake my confidence as conceit, it's not. I had to be better and do more to stay in the game. Daily, I continued to tell myself; I must survive, then hold my chin up a little higher and continued to work harder and be the best I could. I told myself, I have to make it, I'm not a quitter—I am not going to fail. I had to take it; I've endured far worse than a few suggestive looks and people not believing in me. I wanted to be a stockbroker since I was young. I jumped with no clue it would be a hellish struggle. Unfortunately, I came to know the hard way success wasn't going to just ring my doorbell, and a paycheck wouldn't just appear in my mailbox.

I was seriously struggling; my daughter was young. There would be nights I made excuses for her to stay overnight with my parents, to have a warm place to sleep. Many times, I had no heat or electricity; I would pile under blankets in front of my fireplace at night, to not freeze to death in the brutal Wisconsin winters. Times I was so discouraged, out of frustration, I'd say to God, "Really, is this what you have for me?!?" I lost a lot of weight because I didn't eat much. I'd ration food to make sure my daughter would eat because I couldn't afford to feed us both. Though they didn't know how much I was struggling, people around me could tell. They'd say, "You're educated, you can get a job anywhere." There really was no reason that I should have been nearly starving, I could have easily gotten another job. I would imagine hearing their reactions inside my head: "This is ridiculous! You can't feed yourself!" So, I pretended everything was okay, it wasn't. I was in a brutal industry that was set up for me to fail if I believed in the status quo. Making a difference helping people, kept me. I was fortunate to be doing something that my heart desired. People work in jobs by incident, accident, or coincidence and don't work or operate in their mission in life. That would not be my story.

Despite my circumstances, when I helped a client, the inner joy and peace I felt assured me, I had to go through whatever I had to, regardless of how bad things were. Over the years I've been challenged with setbacks and obstacles, but I've stayed the course. Walking in purpose is worth more than any

paycheck. Unfortunately, people would rather stay in a known bondage than pursue an unknown freedom, but not me. Many times, I wanted to give up. With the sexual advances, disrespect, being hungry, cold, and broke, it's a wonder I didn't. The joy and peace are what kept me showing up. Even though people felt what could a young black female possibly have to offer. I knew then: What I had to offer was me!

I was a rare commodity in the financial industry. I realized early that I was blazing a trail. What comforted me then and now; when I wake every morning, I remove myself from the equation and remind myself, this isn't about me, this is for the women who will come after me; I'm on assignment. Someone had to take the persecution, I believed I was the one God trusted to do it. The Bible says, "To whom much is given, much is required." Every time I encountered a hill to climb or a valley to walk, it reinforces what I am supposed to be doing and gives me a better understanding of the message I have to deliver. Those things had to happen. It's never been about the money for me; I'm in it because my heart is in it. Know this: No matter what obstacles life brings your way; you can't give up or let them get in the way of your calling. Desire, drive, and determination are key ingredients for crushing mediocrity. You can do what you want to do and most important, be who God designed and desires you to be!

Bio:
Carmen M. Herrera, award-winning Wealth Advisor, best-selling author, speaker and trainer. She is the Managing Partner of CMHC Wealth Advisors, a leading wealth consulting firm.

Co-author of #1 best-selling book, Mission Unstoppable with Les Brown, and Dr. George C. Fraser. One of the country's most sought after financial experts, Carmen has been featured by media outlets

NBC, FOX, and many more across the country. She toured the U.S. as a featured Financial Advisor for Black Enterprise Magazine's Financial Empowerment Series and The Hip-Hop Summit Action Network's Get Your Money Right series created by Russell Simmons and Dr. Benjamin Chavis.

Carmen is the Co-Founder of the first Black Female Private Equity Firm in Texas, Rhodium Capital Management. She has always been passionate about informing and educating her community. Carmen feels Rhodium will be a conduit for creating and transferring inter-generational wealth in women and minority-owned businesses.

Email: CarmenHerrera@cmhcwealth.com
Website: www.CMHCWealth.com

Charlisa Herriott

Fight, Girl, Fight
By Charlisa Herriott

The hat that I wear now was created from pain but given for purpose.
A hat that adorns adversity but embellishes hope.
A hat that symbolizes discouragement but now drapes with courage.
A hat that I once desired to hide that I now showcase everywhere I go.
A hat as a two time cancer survivor.

For the past 14 years, I've worn this hat, which changed colors, but never design. A hat as a "Fighter," as a "Survivor," as a "Thriver," but, most boldly, as an "Assassinator!" A hat that was given power to kill the enemy; for it to rise no more. This is my hat, which I now wear as a crown. I now reign as Miss Cancer Warrior Queen 2018. A crown given with honor, received by faith, and worn with grace. A crown well-deserved with every cheer when I wear it well.

My "will to fight" all started in May of 2007, when I was in a car accident on my way to visit my mother for Mother's Day weekend. My car hydroplaned, I lost control, and was thrust down the embankment with the front fender down and the back end up. Shortly thereafter, the police arrived and informed me that at the very spot where I crashed and survived, another young lady was tragically killed. A miracle! I knew then that God was with me at every moment.

After going to the ER for further examination, testing, scans, and biopsies, I was diagnosed with a rare form of cancer. I was devastated and became emotionally numb and fearful of the diagnosis. I

106

questioned God, "Why me?" God replied to me saying, "Why not you?" I learned spiritually, that the words I was professing, "God is my provider, and by his stripes I am healed," had to take power and dominion over my situation in order to change my condition in prayer.

The first battle required extensive chemotherapy, the removal of my entire right lung, followed by intense radiation treatments. The road to recovery wasn't easy but it was rewarding. Not even a year after the surgery, God opened up the windows of heaven and poured out a blessing that I did not have room enough to receive. I purchased my first home in the middle of a recession. Who does that? I do! I believed my God, who is able to do exceedingly, abundantly above all I could ever think or imagine. Little did I know that the cancer would return in December of 2016, and the forces that were against me would be more aggressive.

I suffered a stroke, had heart surgery, and, when the pandemic occurred, lost my health insurance while undergoing chemotherapy and radiation treatments. At times, I felt I was going to lose my mind. At that very moment, It was clear that I was fighting for my life.

Through the adversity, the disappointments, and the hurdles I experienced, I discovered the inner strength to rise out of my ashes. I found the courage to rise from the fire set to destroy but ultimately strengthen me. I was strengthened to rise from the smoke that attempted to smother my very breath of life. I learned that what wasn't burned shall live, and I can still breathe. Therefore, I'm blessed to have been favored, chosen, and loved by God; to yet be among the land of the living.

Life is good, and God is greater. Whatever the conditions that surround you, they will not consume you if you only breathe. While your story is still being written, thank God for each day's new script.

Thank God for your fight in your right to breathe. Fight for your voice to be heard. Fight for what you believe. Fight for what you see that God has shown you. Fight to forge forward. Fight strategically. Fight unapologetically. Fight unashamed. Fight with the power of your tongue.

On this day that the Lord has graciously given us, let's be intentional in taking the required dosage for inner healing:

AM DOSAGE: 1 tab of "Thank You Jesus" for giving me another chance, another opportunity, another day to get it right.

MIDDAY DOSAGE: 2 Capsules of "Jesus! I need Your help!" by mouth as needed when fear arises, anxiety increases, calamity occurs, or chaos infuses.

EVENING DOSAGE: 1 drop every 7 hours of "God, You did it Again," when God answers your prayers, when God orders your steps, when God makes a way out of no way, and when God heals you internally.

I desire to live a life that is steady and sturdy. A life that brings forth strength and power. A life that is rewarding and not filled with regrets. A life that springs forth joy, peace, harmony, healing, and wholeness. I don't desire a life of dreadfulness, danger, or destitute of meaning, bearing no fruit. I don't desire to live with rage and being silenced. I don't desire to live on edge, with no sense of direction, flowing through existence without experiencing the joys of living.

I declare to walk in my authenticity, with confidence in knowing who I am, whose I am, and that I was fearfully and wonderfully made. I am "The Healed," made whole, missing nothing, and nothing is broken that God cannot fix to crush it in life!

As the Crushing Chemo Chic, it's not time to sit still and be a spectator. It's not time to blend in with the old and run from the new.

It's not time to play it safe and take the road most familiar. It's not time to remain silent, but forge forward to be heard. It's time to live and breathe again. It's time to wear your crown and fight, girl, fight!

Bio:
Charlisa Herriott, (Coach C) - "The Crushing Chemo Chic," is a Board Certified Life Survivor Strategist who works with female cancer survivors whose life has been crushed with fear to find hope again.

She's a Best-selling Author, Award-Winning Speaker, and TV/radio co-host/podcaster. She has received numerous recognitions such as "Inspirational CEO 2019" and "Miss Cancer Warrior Project 2018."

She has been featured in the 40 Plus & Phenomenal Audio Project, 2019 Words, Wisdom & Winning Women Calendar, 2020 Boss Lady Calendar, the cover of "The Coach" Magazine Series 2020, the "Meet The Coach" Virtual Conference with the Glambitious Magazine, the Black CEO 24 Hours of Entrepreneurship "Secrets of the Champions," and Charge Up Campaign's 2020 Survivors Con Virtual Experience.

"I strive to share my story, experiences, and victories in life in hopes that it may lead one individual to learn, live, and love again. Finally, I'm a licensed minister who loves to minister to the lost, the least, and the lonely."

I can be reached on all social media platforms by the following:
Website: www.crushingchemochic.com
Instagram.com/CharlisaHerriott
Facebook.com/CharlisaHerriott
Facebook.com/CrushingChemoChic
Linkedin.com/in/CharlisaHerriott
Twitter.com/CharlisaHerriot

Joye S. Jackson

It's Time for the Tandem Skydive
By Joye S. Jackson

Have you ever skydived? I haven't!

I have never seen the need to jump out of a perfectly good plane. No emergency equals no jump! In fact, I'm that one person who listens to the flight attendant every time I board a plane. I know where the exits are, I know how to put on my oxygen mask, and I know that my seat can be used as a floatation device. Although I pray each time I fly that I never have to experience any of these emergency procedures, I am aware that they exist for my safety.

'Safety.' That's my favorite word. It has been my greatest strength and my greatest weakness. I would call myself a 'safety sergeant,' a person who believes in order and structure. I like to create a plan and execute it. I don't like surprises or stalls. The idea of failure makes me uneasy, and spontaneity (in most instances) is overrated to me. However, all of that changed in May of 2020.

Let me paint the picture. I had six-year-old twins, and had been married for nearly 11 years with a well-paying, six-figure job creating programs and strategies for an organization. I guess you could say that my plane was soaring high, but one day, my plane hit some turbulence, and I lost my job. This was during the onset of COVID-19, the death of George Floyd, and the shutdown of most cities. My security was gone.

112

I know I shouldn't have depended on my job to that extent. After all, God is my source, and my job and money are just resources, right? But let's be honest. I couldn't recall the safety instructions. I couldn't remember what to do when it counted. You may tell me that lots of people lost their jobs during that time, and you're right, but like many of those people , I wasn't prepared. At the very moment that I felt like I was finally flying comfortably, life said, "OK, Joye, you're going to have to jump!"

Although I had accumulated so many successes, something was missing. That "something" was deposited in me at an early age and 40 years later, it started calling me even louder. Throughout my professional career, I would hear that still, small voice telling me to jump, but I was afraid. To jump required faith. It required strength. It required confidence, and although the rest of the world saw those traits in me, I didn't see them in myself. In June of 2020, however, one month after losing my job, I decided to jump. I started my own business.

Ironically, I never wanted to be an entrepreneur. There was too much uncertainty. As a safety sergeant, anything that is not steady and consistent gives me anxiety, and I had the baggage of self-doubt and fear of rejection weighing heavy on my shoulders. It took hours of preparation, and just like skydiving, I made sure I had all the necessary equipment to jump.

- **The Helmet** – is used for safety, and to prevent permanent damage from head collisions. These were the job applications that I continued to complete if this whole entrepreneur thing didn't work out.

- **The Altimeter** – lets a skydiver know what the current altitude is and when to engage the parachute. This was my detailed business plan.

- **The Activation Device** – automatically pops the parachute at a set altitude. This would be my target market and client list.

113

- **The Goggles** – are used to protect the eyes while skydiving, as well as assist with visibility. This was the vision that I had created for my business.

- **The Parachute** – allows you to float. It is the essence of the experience. For me, this was launching my business and seeing it soar.

As I surveyed the checklist, I knew I had taken all the right steps to safely jump out of the plane and start my own business. The only thing left to do was jump. Again I heard that still, small voice encouraging me to step out. Fear began to creep in. What happens if my equipment malfunctions? What happens if I fail? These questions weighed me down so much that I procrastinated for four more months.

Finally, on October 31, 2020, I decided to jump. I prayed, closed my eyes, and jumped out of the plane. It was exhilarating! I made my business public, launched my website, printed business cards, and compiled videos and social media. All my preparation had paid off, but just like skydiving, I started the free fall. I couldn't catch my breath. It felt like I was going to plummet head-first into the ground.

To my surprise, my 'parachute' didn't open as I believed it would. Fear and doubt surfaced again. "This was a bad idea," I thought. "I must have been out of mind to think that I could be an entrepreneur." I was about to accept my fate and return to a regular job when my parachute opened, and I started to float!

In that moment I realized the Lord had invited me to join Him in a tandem skydive the entire time. The business idea was His all along, and as the perfect instructor, He was with me all the way through. All this time I thought I was jumping alone, but He was guiding me through the whole thing, from the preparation, to the exit, to the freefall, and even piloting the canopy. When I believed that I was about to jump by myself, I was never truly alone.

My prayer is that you will discover the Greatest Instructor is fully involved in your endeavors, training and equipping you for the jump, and when you find the courage to step out, you'll know what it's like to jump in tandem with Him!

Bio:

Joye Jackson is known for her commitment to empowering others to reach their full potential through her coaching, workshops, and professional speaking. She has over 18 years' experience in learning/development, project management, facilitation, strategic planning, and communications. She works with women who are ready to step into their greater purpose and overcome the things that are holding them back from reaching their goals – fear, questions, lack of time, lack of support and more. Together they chart a pathway to what's next for them. Speaking of Joye's mission is to help women fulfill their purpose through her coaching, workshops and speaking. Together, through strategy sessions, they create customized action plans that help her clients incrementally achieve the goals they have set.

Connect with Joye on all social media platforms at Speaking of Joye or on her website at www.speakingofjoye.com.

B. Jacqueline Jeter

In My DNA
By B. Jacqueline Jeter

There are four names on my birth certificate. I was told my brother named me after three of his favorite girlfriends. My last name is the fourth. One thing to note in regard to my names, is that common, average or mediocre is not of record.

I know that I was created for greatness and meant to be here. I was born to parents who were much older than my friends' parents- my mother was 46 and my dad 52 when I was born. Back in the late 60's, this would have been a death sentence because it was said that babies born to mothers at such a late age would be cognitively challenged. However , God created me on the other end of the spectrum, because He made me brilliant. Please don't think I'm being pompous; I've just learned how to crush mediocrity and own my prowess.

While I had the most amazing, supportive, and encouraging family and was provided experiences that exposed me to priceless, diverse opportunities throughout my childhood, I found out quickly that those outside my bubble of protection were not as ready to be introduced to my genius.

I managed to walk boldly and authentically for a while until I was confronted by a bully. While comforting me, my father gave me what I call my 'resilience mantra.' He told me to dry my eyes, and remember that, "they may pick at you today, but they will work for you tomorrow." These words of wisdom were with me through secondary school, college, and still today as I navigate the corporate world.

Mediocrity is a state of mind. You have to tell your mind who you are. When I was younger, I was told there was nothing I could not accomplish. Because of this , whenever I was challenged with the mediocre thoughts of others, told something had not been done before, or given a low expectation of success, I knew that I was going to crush the odds.

There have been times that I allowed myself to be beaten down and even beat myself down because of someone else's opinions and stereotypes. I spent years blending in, going with the flow, and downplaying my true essence. However , while I thought I was hiding, others saw my brilliance.

One of the turning points in my life that broke me out of this assimilated state happened after I was laid off by a corporation which I worked for over 24 years. There I was, in my late 40's, starting over. Everyone knew who I was. My name was known, and I was established. I was in the sweet spot of my career. I was comfortable! Then, boom; due to a reorganization, a couple thousand of us were gifted to the unemployment pool.

It was this cage- rattling experience that forced me to rediscover my uniqueness and brilliance. It was time to embrace all of who I was - every quirk, every idiosyncrasy. After I left that career job and before I landed another role, I took several months to reacquaint with myself .

The first thing I did to crush the state of mediocrity I was in was take inventory. I wrote down everything I had accomplished in the past 24 years while I was at that corporation. It blew my mind. I hadn't realized I had accomplished so much and acquired so many skill sets. Now, I knew where I was going because I knew where I had been.

Number two, I changed my language and my associations. I had fallen into the habit of using limited mindset verbiage. I intentionally wrote

119

out affirmations, created a life mission statement, and developed goals that supported me to accomplish said mission statement. I also ensured I surrounded myself with the right people. Needless to say, some naysayers were moved from the VIP section to nosebleed seats of my life.

The third thing I did to crush mediocrity was put action behind those goals. Before being evicted from my work nirvana, and in addition to my core job as a scientist, I became a certified job plus coach Job Plus Coach. I pursued additional certifications and created a coaching platform for young, pharmaceutical professionals.

By doing these three things, I re-established that brilliant, nine year-old kid that my dad encouraged to keep striving.

There is a battle for excellence within each of us. It is that very battle for brilliance versus the muck of mediocrity that pushes me forward and should push you forward too. It is time to remind yourself that mediocrity is not your place of residence. If you're living on Mediocrity Street, it's time to change your address. I don't mean get a pod or call a moving company. I mean leave behind everything that keeps you in the low vibration of average that is a mediocrity mindset. Get your bag or whatever you need, and move to your place of excellence. Remember the Jeffersons? They moved on up to the East side to a deluxe apartment in the sky. They used to live in a neighborhood in the suburbs, but when George's cleaners took off, he couldn't live there anymore because the mentality of his surroundings could no longer contain his success. You cannot stay on Mediocrity Street and still excel. Remember, it's a state of mind.

When you crush mediocrity, you avail yourself to be a trailblazer, a world changer, and a legacy builder. You cannot lay down with mediocrity and rise to be great.

I remind myself daily that there is excellence, greatness, brilliance in my DNA. There are kings and queens in my DNA. There is ingenuity, creativity, and entrepreneurship in my DNA. There are physicians, lawyers, educators, and scientists in my DNA. The mind, the breath, and the life of a champion is in my DNA. In my DNA is success, amazingness, anointing, power, and might; but nowhere is there mediocrity in my DNA.

Bio:

Transformational Growth Strategist. Encouragement Ambassador. International speaker. Four-time Amazon best-selling co-author. B Jacqueline Jeter is CEO and Founder of Grow, Lead and Prosper™ which focuses on equipping women to conquer limited mindsets personally, professionally, and spiritually so they can grow from a point of stagnation to their place of purpose and boldly show up to impact and influence the spheres for which they were created and destined. She also empowers small groups to identify, address, and conquer challenges so they can transform to highly performing teams

Jacqueline is a certified Vision Coach and celebrated Independent Certified Leadership Coach, Teacher and Speaker with the John Maxwell Team. She holds several degrees and certificates and boasts an over 28 year career as a consummate pharmaceutical veteran in global drug research and development program management.

Email:	jacqueline@growleadandprosper.com
Facebook:	Grow Lead and Prosper; B Jacqueline Jeter
Instagram:	@growleadandprosper; @bjacquelinejeter
Website:	www.growleadandprosper.com

Cassandra R. Johnson

Running for My Life Never Losing Faith
By Cassandra R. Johnson

I thought I had it all together when I packed up and moved from New Jersey to Atlanta in August of 2011. In reality, I was hanging on for dear life. I was so used to being "successful" to others that even when things were falling apart, I convinced myself I still had it together. You know the saying "Fake it 'til you make it?" At this point, I was faking it because everything was heading south.

By June of 2012, everything started unravelling. The coaching company I worked with went under. I was living off unemployment and my 401K. In the midst of a recession, I had to scramble to get a job. Wait, what? Hold up! I was that girl who always had a six figure job, real-estate investments, and a couple of side hustles. I was always successful, "doing the most," and working around the clock. If I didn't like a job, I quit and had another one in less than 30 days. I had gone through four layoffs in my career and always bounced back. However, this time, I didn't bounce back, I crashed and burned.

The stress was overwhelming. I was used to working out at the gym to relieve stress, but this time, I had to let that go because I couldn't afford it. A friend of mine introduced me to Black Girls Run, which was huge in Atlanta at the time. That was in September of 2012 and the first time I even thought about running in over 25 years. I laughed at first and thought, "Oh God, what am I doing? " but when my feet hit the pavement, I felt like a weight had been lifted. I huffed and puffed my way through three miles, running a little, walking a lot, but I discovered two things: a new way to relieve stress, and a new tribe of women who became a source of strength for me as I navigated through my mess. At that moment, I was running for my life, and God had orchestrated the whole thing.

By December of 2012, I was completely broke and couldn't afford to pay rent on my own. I sold nearly everything; furniture, fur, purses, skis, shoes, you name it. I had over $40K in credit card and IRS debt and had several mortgages, one of which I had to stop paying altogether and try to short sell before it went to foreclosure. I picked up a contract gig, which I landed on the spot, but it only paid about a third of what I was used to making. I moved in with a friend for a while until I was able to get a job making enough money to get my own place again. Talk about humbling. I hadn't depended on anyone since college, and there I was over 20 years later with a roommate. Through it all, I stayed humble, kept searching for a better job, and continued running. Every chance I got, I ran. I felt so broken at times. I had complete meltdowns on the pavement. Thank God for my tribe because they were right there praying me through my mess, and I needed lots of prayer.

A break came…or so I thought. I landed a job that paid six figures like I was used to making, but I was fired nine days later for a very weak reason, and I had to threaten legal action to get paid for the time I worked. To top it off, the court was about to foreclose on the house I stopped paying the mortgage on because the short sale fell through. At that point, I broke. I felt like I hit rock bottom, and all I could do was drop to my knees… But God.

The weekend before my foreclosure hearing, I got an unexpected FedEx package from the court. Thankfully, they pushed the hearing back four months, and I was able to sell the house before it went to foreclosure.

One thing was clear throughout my mess, especially at that moment: God was with me, my tribe was with me, and my break would soon come…and it did. Four months later, I landed a job that was tailor made for me. It's funny how I landed it. I was so broke the day of my interview, I didn't have enough money to print out my work to take with me. I was also limping because of an injury. What did I do? I carried my old 17" laptop under my arm, limped into the interview, opened it up, and did my thing. The interviewer knew I did not come to play and was very impressed. I had three more interviews after that and sealed the deal. I knew I would because I knew God was guiding me the entire way.

After nearly three years of mess, I was finally back on my own feet, on a new path. I discovered a new love, running, gained a new tribe of praying, sister friends, and embarked on a new career fully dependent on God. To this day, God has restored everything I lost and more. Now, I get to share the lessons I learned from my mess with you.

- **Stop "Doing The Most"** – Stop trying to live a lifestyle to impress others that makes a mess of your own life. What God has for you is for you. Period.

- **Do Something New** – Find that one thing that will help you better navigate through the stress of life. For me, it was running. For you, it may be something else.

- **Find Your Tribe** – Have a trusted group of friends who will be a constant source of strength for you in good and bad times.

- **Make God Your Source**….for everything.

I went from "doing the most" to please others to "doing what I love" to please God and restore others. Now I coach other women to do the same.

Bio:

Cassandra R Johnson is the CEO of Destined To Be Great, an executive coaching company focused on helping professional women reduce stress, improve their time management skills, and ultimately create a personalized "Life Harmony Plan." She is a Certified Professional Coach and Energy Leadership Master Practitioner. In addition, she is a Sales and Marketing Professional with over 20 years' experience in brand marketing and consulting with several Fortune 500 companies.

As an advocate for empowering women, Ms. Johnson is a contributing author to two other books: *Leadership; Helping Others to Succeed* and *Wealthy Direct Sales Women.*

She is an avid runner who has completed 30 half marathons and 4 full marathons in 22 different states.

Ms. Johnson holds a B.S. Degree from North Carolina State University and an M.B.A. from Duke University.

To learn more about Destined To Be Great, visit www.destined2bgreat.comor email Coach Cassandra at cassandra@destined2bgreat.com.

Erica Lane

Control Your Financial Destiny - Take Your Power Back From 'They'

By Erica Lane

It would have been comfortable to settle into the role that "they" created for me. After all, what's wrong with working a great job? Absolutely nothing, and don't let anyone tell you otherwise if that's what you truly want. However, I knew at a young age the drum of my heartbeat was to entrepreneurship. This isn't to say that there weren't times when striving for success got hard and the ease that settling provided wasn't tempting, but the challenges are what have formed me to create the impact that I make today. I always followed this particular rule: "Go for it, no matter what 'they' say or do!"

Striving to overcome mediocrity may sometimes mean you're the only one in your circle pushing back against the status quo. I remember at a business summit listening to a powerful motivational speaker. Not only was she a powerhouse on stage, had a lengthy list of accolades, was wealthy, and looked like me, she was also humble and approachable. I was inspired by her story! I knew if she could bounce back from her situation, so could I! Some of my closest friends were with me at that event, and I told them that I was going to "rebuild my finances beyond what I had lost and become a full-time successful entrepreneur again." They responded, "You are a single mother, whose fiancé left you not long ago." "You just got a great job that you are great at, with amazing benefits. You should just stick to that." "Don't waste your money starting a new business. You may have done it before, but remember how hard the fall was. Take your failure as a sign." For two seconds I shook my head in agreement, but then I remembered that if you could

130

build something once, you can rebuild it even from pieces! While that emotional and financial fall was, in fact, exponentially traumatizing, there was a purpose behind it, and I had no right to surrender to the fear of failing. In that moment, I decided I would walk directly into that purpose. I learned how to rebuild my life, save, restore my credit from 400s to 700s, budget my money, make strong investments and build a new, successful business. My experience is the foundation of the strategies I teach women around the world to this very day!

The difference between dreaming and accomplishing those dreams is action. I knew I had to act, or I was going to stay in the same cycle of mediocrity. Very few people accomplish their goals because of societal influences that pressure people to abide by the norm. Society has conditioned us to be content with our average lives, and this affects our excellence. Of course, I don't wholeheartedly believe my friends' comments came from a bad place. In fact, I think they, like many family and friends, believed they were protecting me from an unnecessary failure while bringing me back to reality. Also, bursting my bubble kept them comfortable with their own insecurities and mediocrity. A word to the wise- stop trying to stay small to keep everyone around you comfortable.

I pushed through mediocrity and made myself (and honestly a few friends who were not ready for growth) uncomfortable. The following tips are how I did it:

Top 5 Tips to Push Through Mediocrity with Power

1. Stop Doubting Yourself

Doubt does more harm than good to your dreams. It comes in varying forms. You see yourself doubting everything, from your intelligence to your capability, which affects dreams more than you realize. If you constantly doubt yourself, you will never take on a new opportunity because you will always have a perfect excuse. Rather than continue listening to that voice of doubt, why not choose the voice of value? Doubting yourself is underselling your worth and capabilities, which constantly leads to mediocrity. You need to reject the idea that you are not good enough, because you are.

2. Find Your Purpose

There needs to be a reason why you do what you do or sell what you sell. If you are an entrepreneur, your business needs to have a purpose, because it has no substance otherwise. Your purpose is the reason you choose to continue even when things get rough. However, finding a goal is not an easy task as it takes a lot of introspection. Take your time to decide what exactly your purpose really is, and use hard work and dedication to follow through.

3. Get Out Of Your Comfort Zone

You need to challenge yourself constantly if you want to rise above the standard. The good thing is you don't have to take huge leaps. You can start with measured steps. Remember - the race to overcome mediocrity isn't a sprint, it's a marathon. Consistency wins!

4. Never Settle On Things You Really Want

My success is set on the backbone of numerous failures and challenges. Failure is not a bad thing if you learn a lesson from it. See it as a guide on what not to do. When things get tough, it is essential to never settle, even if it looks like a comfortable decision. Wake up with the mantra that you will never settle. When one way doesn't work, try another!

5. Don't Give In To Fear

Letting your fears govern your choices is where the problem resides. Fear cripples you and keeps you from making decisions. Fear will discourage you from taking risks in your life. When you don't give in to fear, you allow yourself to experience life and do remarkable things. If someone had told me when I was young that I would be an international speaker, money coach, and author, I wouldn't have believed them. Yet, I took the risks anyway!

Get more tips at iAmEricaLane.com

Bio:

The Money Elevation Strategist has developed an exceptional money management approach, which enabled her to triple her income in three years. The founder of the School of Money Elevation, Award-winning Money Coach, Best-selling Author, International Speaker, Conference Creator, and Book Anthology Visionary. Her definition of success is to inspire women to change their money habits and, therefore, their financial outcomes. Her clients develop the clarity and fearlessness to achieve their goals and tell the money story of their dreams, on their terms. As a natural motivational speaker, she empowers women to recognize their value. Erica specializes in helping women build, restore and elevate their money through budgeting.

Her mission is to focus women to be savvy about the decisions they make with their money and business, plus achieve mastery over it, and leave a significant legacy for generations to come!

Freebie!   thebudgetstrategies.com
Follow Erica on Facebook/Instagram/Linkedin @iAmEricaLane
Website: iAmEricaLane.com
Classes: schoolofmoneyelevation.com

Dr. Bridget A. Leonard

Living My Best Life: Crushing Goals
By Dr. Bridget A. Leonard RN

How many times have you thought to yourself, "I wish my life were different. I wish I could have been somebody else?" I've thought this to myself many times. I wanted to figure out if God was truly such a great God, why did he give me the life he did? I'm Dr. B, and I want to take you on a journey inside of my life so that you can understand where I came from and why I appreciate where I am today by crushing goals every chance I get.

Children are innocent yet vulnerable. Unfortunately, it is hard for me to remember times in my life where I could be an innocent child. My life was uncomplicated until around the age of ten. I was living the American Dream: I had a mom, a dad, and a dog named Sambo. I lived in a house with a white picket fence. However, life as I knew it began going downhill on April 26, 1980. This was the day that my dad committed suicide. Four days before my tenth birthday. It still feels unreal that he is gone; that my cloak of protection left me naked and vulnerable to the nuances of this world.

After my dad died, I went to live with my mom full time, and I became exposed to a totally different type of world. What a lot of people do not know is although my mother birthed me, I'm not sure if she knew how to love me. My mom was a beautiful woman. She had a heart of gold, but she wasn't always mother material. My mother suffered from depression, constant mood swings, alcoholism, and drug dependency. As a child, and even now as an adult, I don't understand why I had to work so hard simply to get her approval. I just wanted her to love me.

136

I genuinely believe if my mother had shown me and others that she loved me unconditionally, my life would have been much different. It's mind-boggling how predators prey on the innocent when they see an opportunity to pounce. One of those opportunities was, sadly, sexual molestation by multiple adults including older cousins, a trusted female babysitter, and older men that were considered to be family friends. I was lucky in those many encounters that it was always just a kiss, a touch, or a creepy look. It was never actual intercourse, but it still scarred me and tainted me for life. I often blamed my dark skin and big lips for my troubles. As the darkest female in my family, I thought I was being punished for not looking like everyone else; as if I had a target in the middle of my head.

I looked for love constantly. I wanted someone to love me for me and not want anything in return. I thought I found that in my first love, but that experience only exposed me to raising two children by the age of 17 and the addition of physical, verbal, and mental abuse to my sorry list of accomplishments. As I felt life couldn't get worse, my mother ran around the house searching for me with a loaded shotgun with hopes of killing me during one of her drug-induced rages when I was 17. She shot my uncle instead.

It's crazy that I allowed all of this to happen to me considering I had been a straight A student; book smart but not street smart. Yet, after I had two kids and was dealing with an abusive mom and boyfriend, I chose to drop out of high school. In truth, I didn't feel life was worth living. For years I dealt with depression. My first attempt at suicide was at 15. It was silly of me to think I would die from a bottle of Tylenol. Yet, I tried again two more times, and as you can see, those attempts were also unsuccessful.

Fortunately, I began to turn my life around. It took the tragic deaths of my mom and infant child, and my job at McDonalds for me to realize that my life was worth living. My life served a purpose, and I was still alive to help others. After these events, I realized I needed to be a better mom and better person by releasing the demons of my past. I didn't want my kids to struggle to find words to write in my obituary, like I did with my own mother. I also realized making $3.35 an hour at McDonalds was not going to fully provide for my family. I wanted and needed to do more.

I went back to school and became a LPN in 1996, which ignited a fire within my soul to practice nursing. I went on to become a RN in 2001, obtain six college degrees including my Doctorate, hold executive level nursing positions, be an active member on many boards, and be heavily involved in the community. I created my own company in which I am a certified life coach, providing leadership and motivational speaking as well as programs that primarily focus on helping broken women break down barriers, find their purpose in life, and create platforms where they can excel.

Today, I am proud to have the honor of being Dr. B, and my personal mission statement is to positively impact at least one person every day through words, thoughts, or actions. I want to leave three tips that helped me to understand my value and my purpose to this world. The first tip is to seek professional help for any type of mental illness or mental distress without delay. The second tip is to live your best life and do things that put a smile on your face. You can't pour from an empty cup. The third tip is to take control of the pen that is your life and write your own damn chapters. Don't let society define what you can control.

Live your best life-crushing goals, and don't you dare let your past dictate your future!

Bio:

From CNA to Chief Nursing Officer, Dr. Bridget Leonard didn't allow her past to dictate her future. Her transparency, courage, and motivation empowers others to know anything is possible when committed to doing the work. CEO of Bridget Leonard Enterprises, LLC she tailors her efforts to helping people reach their highest potential through coaching, professional speaking, mentoring, and professional development. Dr. Leonard serves as a life coach to many who are on a mission to live their best life, authentically and unapologetically. She is committed to helping people identify strategic goals, tear down potential barriers, and develop strategies to make their dreams a reality. From motivating the masses, team building and engagement, to employee recognition and professional advancement opportunities, Dr. Leonard is sure to leave a mark on the hearts and minds of attendees through her speaking and nuggets of wisdom.

Contact her at info@BridgetLeonard.com, get free eBook @ bit.ly/Meet_DrB

Tina D. Lewis

Pivot. Position. Prosper!
By Tina D. Lewis

2020 is my year!

Well, that's what I proclaimed! I and many others I know. We even had vision boards and girl gatherings in 2019 to discuss exactly how it would go. I knew If I did exactly what I did for my clients and myself last year, with just a few minor tweaks, with less procrastination, and firing on all cylinders, 2021 would be a piece of cake! My goal was to earn $5 Million, author ten books, mentor 20 clients to $100k in 6-12 months, launch three new revenue-generating platforms, invest in real estate, travel to Croatia, Paris, and Dubai, to name a few. I had BHAGs (Big Hairy Audacious Goals)!

NEWSFLASH: March 13, 2020: President Donald Trump declared a U.S. national emergency, and on March 15th, the CDC warns against large gatherings of 50 or more.

WAIT! I'm THE Bottomline Queen. I crush mediocrity! I multiply the revenue and profits of entrepreneurs and small business owners! I Mentor, Coach, Train, Teach, Speak, Network, Brunch, Dinner and . . . GATHER for a living! (happy face)

I must admit, initially, I was devastated but remained hopeful. "This shouldn't last for more than a few weeks," I thought. However, 48 hours later, on March 17th: the virus was present in all 50 states, and every day there were new discoveries and even more restrictions.

Even though I was frustrated and in disbelief, I remembered a billionaire mentor of mine saying, "Tina, if you want to become wealthy, find out where the world is going and get there during the first wave. You don't have to be first; just get there. When you do that, you will never have to worry about money again! Simply BE the solution to a need!"

PIVOT: I was invited to a Zoom conference call hosted by a top nephrologist who called on community leaders, influencers, healthcare providers, pastors, and anyone who had an interest in purveying the proper education and information to the communities in need. I have a genuine concern and compassion for people and am trained as a Physician Assistant, so I was "in the room!" I wanted to donate my services in any capacity. On approximately our third call, one of the medical clinic administrators stated that they and other clinics needed masks and other medical supplies. I went from listening intently as a participant to interrupting the conversation, as a moderator requesting his contact information, assuring him that I could fulfill the order and would call him afterward. Under normal circumstances, I would say, I have no idea "why" or "where" that came from, but as a Faith walker, I simply trusted God.

In the midst of the "pandemic" and all the discoveries about the virus, physicians, first responders, healthcare workers, and the American people felt scared and unsafe. Protective gear such as masks, gloves, eye gear, facial protective shields, hand sanitizer, alcohol pads, surgical gowns, and many other medical supplies was extremely scarce and in high demand. No one expected a pandemic, so stocks were insufficient, and no shipments from overseas were admitted into the United States (especially China because that was where the "virus" was said to have originated).

POSITION: We did some research, made a few phone calls, and by the grace of God, Protective Gear Unlimited was birthed! It was a challenge to procure the merchandise, but we prevailed. We had masks, gloves, face shields, and gowns.

June 2020, the number of people who had contracted the virus reached 2 million! Our economy remained strained and shut down as 22 million Americans were unemployed. (Praise Break) Amid a pandemic, I was able to position myself and my business to thrive. With just two orders from the clinics, more than half of my year's income was replaced. HALLELUJAH!

As the world began to accept that wearing masks, facial protective clothing, working from home, and virtual meetups were the norm, many entrepreneurs and business owners realized they needed to pivot. Mastering strategies, blueprints, launches, webinars, and collaborations to replace the lost income first and then supersede that was a priority. There is nothing having the expertise and skillset to build a system that would provide CPR to a financially choking entity! It's my superpower!

PROSPER: You see, I had made my plans, wrote them in ink, and was ready to execute, but God prepared something different. Not only did He have a ram in the bush, but He also provided a vehicle where I earned almost $50,000 in 60 days. That's not even the best part. I was also able to help my friends and clients earn income too! Yes! Even during an economic debacle! (Praise dance and shuffle right here!)

Crushing mediocrity has been FULL STEAM AHEAD. Even though I'm trained as a healthcare professional, a PA, I discovered very early on that I was chronically unemployable. I worked at a clinic, and while working there, I started a housekeeping service which was my first taste of entrepreneurship. I was smitten and have had numerous businesses ever since. Some were a bust, others were profitable, and the later ones were explosive!

144

I have a gift, and I don't take it for granted. I can take any business model, from a lemonade stand, a makeup artist, a teacher, a nurse, a speaker, an author, a printing shop to a Fortune 100, 500, or 5000 company and drastically multiply its revenue and profit margin (if I can't create a blueprint or strategy to enhance your bottom line, then there is none). I've been called the "Cash Flow Catalyst" by the Small Business Expo, the Queen of Rapport & Recruiting, an Expert, and even a Magician. As long as the results are substantiated, I'll take it!

I know it's uncomfortable in this season. You may be terrified, or maybe you're thriving. The bottom line is, where do you go from here? If you don't know. Let me tell you! UP! No matter where you are, where you've been, the direction is up!

Bio:

Tina D. Lewis is a 3-Time International Best-Selling Author, philanthropist, blazing Sales and Marketing Expert, the CEO of Royalty Coaching LLC, and the Catalyst of The 6-Figure Incubator, a multi-functional powerhouse execution, known for producing six-figure commodities for quality entrepreneurs; built for exponential success. Affectionately known as the "Bottom Line" Queen, Tina specializes in creating tangible wealth opportunities in the lives of both vetted and budding professionals, helping them eliminate minuscule thinking, stagnant business reflexes, and one-dimensional branding. She has helped many entrepreneurs, including an exclusive women's branch from her non-profit organization. Her mission is to help entrepreneurs overcome the delusion of underperformance, shift their mindset, and gain the clarity necessary to transform their businesses forever. Her Mantra is simple:

After it is all said and done, the most important question is... "What's your Bottom Line?"
Tina D. Lewis. Revenue Generator. Executor. Mogul.

Virginia Dale Manning

All Single Mothers Need to Wear a Triple D

By Virginia Dale Manning, LPC-S

"She is clothed with strength and dignity and she laughs without fear of the future"
Proverbs 31:25

On July 13, 1988, my struggle began.

A compelling statistic declares, "Only 40 percent of teen mothers finish high school." (ncsl.org, 2013).

As a junior at Central Senior High School, I managed to maintain my grades but ended up sitting out that year as a clarinet player in the Jaguar marching band.

By senior year, my grades had dropped significantly. I started skipping school two weeks at a time. I continued to lose my spot on the field for the Friday night football games. My strength had faded.

At 23 years old, I had four children with two different men and was a chronic single parent. My overwhelming daily cycle spun with work, school, kids. This never-ending hamster wheel of frustration and exhaustion took over my life.

My kids and I wake up at six AM, dressing and struggling to make it out the door by seven AM. Sluggishly, we walk around the corner in unison to Pietzsch-MacArthur Elementary and South Park Middle School just in time for their free breakfast. With my loaded backpack in tow, I swiftly strut five more blocks to Lamar University.

I'm just in time for the eight AM Psychology lecture. I flop down and inhale a deep breath, exhale heat. Focus. Three lecture classes later, undergrad study for the day is complete.

At two PM, I walk back home, hurriedly dress for Market Basket bakery/deli, wolf down a big bowl of fruity pebbles and milk, and dash out the door, across the street to serve others on my feet until seven PM.

Next, I get the kids from daycare. Thank God our Section 8 house is near everything we need.

 We walk home in unison feeling like yoyos, happy and sad. Yes, I can kick these worn soles clear across the room. Now, get the kids READY! Eat, homework, bathe, school clothes... SET!

Tomorrow, same channel... GO!

Another compelling statistic, "Single moms are one of the most disadvantaged groups in the U.S.- nearly 30% of their families live under the poverty line..." (US Census).

Success comes with an expensive price tag when you don't know what to wear.

Society sends the daunting message that if a single mother happens to evolve into a pillar of success, she must wear an "S" on her chest.

149

WOMEN CRUSHING MEDIOCRITY

As a single mother, I wore the honorable badge of "Triple D." I was not born average. My lifestyle bred me into a No Ordinary Woman.

Virginia's Law Book of Strength states, "Statistics are made just so that they can be defied." Since the age of 16 in 1988, my purpose on God's Earth has been to **defy** society's conception that I would not complete high school.

Twelfth grade almost took me out. A light bulb shined when I glared into the angelic eyes of my baby girl. The twinkle in her eyes pushed my spirit up, and my conscious regained focus on what I had to do to set her up for future success.

My journey through high school was tough. Getting up early, feeding a baby, walking to the bus stop, soaking up knowledge all day, returning home, caring for a baby, studying to pass classes, preparing for college; all of those struggles were not easy.

I was wise to take a 360 degree direction and flip every single negative into an astounding, positive action for a strong finish.

The road that led to a lifestyle of success had only begun. It takes the power of gratitude to keep the engines revved up. Every time my subconscious directed me back to "teenage mothers drop out of school," I gave thanks for how far I had made it.

I had a lot of outside interventions, such as Minnie Lee, who wasn't playing with me about finishing school. I connected with some awesome teachers who saw my potential, and have been blessed with the favor of God, which has always been present in my life. I still thank each influence, seen and unseen, that came between my failures.

Life's trials and traumas could easily open a sink-hole of self-esteem that was too deep to see my way out of. My self-worth was so low and heavy that the only direction I could hold my head was down.

Over 25 years ago, I bumped into a friend's mother at the grocery store. I'm positive she was well aware of my abusive baby daddy. She abruptly stopped my cart and said, "Why are you looking down at the devil? Hold your head up!" Her voice permeated my soul to an eye-opening awakening that I needed to **define** who I was.

I started a self-identity assessment to reflect on negatives I let define my life and recalibrate positive definitions of who God says I am.

My core values built courage to break through barriers, perseverance to never give up, and self- love to build the foundation that my children and I deserved.

For all single mothers, the future holds endless opportunities, possibilities, and wealth. Determination holds the link between sinking below expectations and rising above to success. Every day is a day to refuse to let any obstacle win.

In my earlier years, I developed skills of strength and dignity. The control was up to me.

In a life of **determination**, a keen superpower is the ability to control negative distractors. Distractors will steal your progress, and cause you to live in fear.

Virginia's Law Book of Strength gives direction to establish disciplines and guidelines of greatness. If you don't plan for success, you're likely to fail at anything you attempt.

Fast forward to the present me. If you already follow me on social media or participate in my membership, you can see that my struggles as a single mother have opened plenty of doors for my dream lifestyle to manifest.

My life has been challenging but in no way is it average or ordinary.

Wear a Triple D.

Bio:

Virginia Dale Manning, LPC-S radiates as a Licensed Professional Counselor and Licensed Chemical Dependency Counselor. She has over 18 combined years of experience in education and therapy. She leads as the CEO of GinMan Consulting, a therapy-based company. She also founded Prosper Under Pressure, a community of empowered women living a lifestyle of calm and confidence.

Serving as a powerful and authentic mental wellness advocate, she stands firm against stigma. Her mission evolves through sharing her knowledge and the vital resources necessary to help you live your dream life. Her passion happens through motivating, inspiring, guiding and supporting others to overcome life's common challenges.

Get to know Virginia on Facebook and Instagram @ginmanconsulting and @prosperunderpressure

Dive deeper into the many dynamics of Virginia at ginmanconsulting.com and pupprofessionalwomen.com

Most importantly if you are a single mother… Become a part of the private affiliation The Single Factor at bit.ly/thesinglefactor. The experience is explosive!

LaTalya M. Palmer

Born for More: Not Even Generational Bondage Can Limit You!
By LaTalya M. Palmer

The most challenging yet rewarding breakthroughs of my life was breaking free from the mental, emotional, and financial shackles of poverty. The most impactful shift in mindset was the understanding that I was not bound to the conditions I was born into. I now lay claim to my birthright of success and abundance.

Growing up, very few people in my immediate family got up in the morning to go to work. I had two aunts that I remember having a job and one cousin that owned his own business. Everyone else waited for a check in the mail. I was born into generational welfare and learned early on that someone else would care for my needs. I grew dependent on external rescue, and while I didn't feel poor, I did feel a sense of helplessness. Everyone around me seemed to acquiesce to the struggle. You either complained about what wasn't working, settled for what you had, or found a way to work the system to get more. Conversations were about how many children you needed to have to get the maximum amounts of food stamps and cash assistance, tips on how to keep case workers from coming to your house, or cautioning the newbies not to provide workers with the name or address of their child's father. There were no other spoken hopes, dreams, or ambitions.

By the age of 14, I started working a summer job and fell in love with going to cash the check and receiving money in my hands. I found a love for being in the work world because I caught on easily, felt smart, and needed money for school clothes. As I neared 18, I didn't know how I was going to make it in the world without a welfare check. I remember when my mother took me to the welfare office and told me we now had the same case worker. It was a very intrusive experience. They wanted to know everything about me, and if I didn't fit the criteria, I would be disqualified. I remember feeling nervous that I wouldn't fit in their box. Their box that would require me to sign over my rights to a full, free, healthy, abundant life. At that time, welfare limited the types of food you could buy with food stamps, what doctor you could go to, and where you lived because of the minimal cash assistance provided. A father's name couldn't appear on your birth certificate, and you had minimal freedom to decide where your child was educated. You could only have a limited amount in your savings account. I didn't worry about credit scores, banking, saving for a home and the like because I didn't understand how any of it applied to me.

In my early 20's, I decided to walk away. The case worker threatened a house inspection because my daughter wasn't receiving welfare benefits. Her father provided for her. It was an extremely demeaning experience. I left her office determined not to return. I vividly remember struggling to envision my life without public assistance. I couldn't imagine my life without food stamps to buy food and money to help me pay rent, move to a new place, and buy furniture. Despite this, there was something within that wouldn't allow me to settle for that existence. I felt trapped, but I heard whispers of possibilities that encouraged me to believe in a reality I'd never seen.

I found a job at a factory and went on to secure small jobs until I landed on a career that I was great at and a gift that I am in love with. Today, I am a deputy chief in procurement. I've consulted and served as an empowerment trainer for human service agencies and vulnerable populations as well as a life coach, author, and speaker for women who are moving through adversities.

I make the conscious decision to grow at each level of life. Each level comes with spiritual, emotional, and mental healing. My best days are in front of me, and had I not walked out of that welfare office decades ago, I wouldn't have had these fulfilling experiences. I recognize that I have many miles to go, but I am grateful for the journey I've walked.

You may have been born into a generational pattern of limitation, but understand that you don't have to be a victim to it. You're not your past, and you have the capacity to create the life you deserve. You have the power to break free from victimhood, blaming others for what you don't have, not taking ownership of your experience, and staying trapped in an experience that doesn't speak to your greatness.

Here are some tips to help you break through:

1. **Renew your mind** – only you have the power to change your thoughts and beliefs. You can pray for renewal of your mind, but you must be willing to open it and do the work to maintain a renewed mental state. Begin feeding your mind with empowering, uplifting, healthy messages about yourself and your ability.

2. **Create a new vision for your life**- confess where you are feeling lack, resolve to release it, and visualize a greater quality of life.

3. **Form a power network**- determine who can help lift you to your next level and who you can help get to theirs. Find a way to network and connect.

4. **Speak life into the dry bones**- examine the uninspired, scarce areas of your life and speak good into them

5. **Begin taking action toward your vision** – create your plan and take immediate action. Consistency is key to forming healthy habits and getting the results you want.

Believe in yourself that you were born to live a greater quality of life and ignite the dreams of your heart. Whether you are feeling limited in money, talent , resources, opportunities, or love, you can crush mediocrity and expand your territory.

Bio:

LaTalya Palmer, The Dream Igniter has been in the empowerment industry for 20+ years. She is a certified empowerment trainer and Law of Attraction coach that helps others turn their adversities into fuel to achieve their dreams. She has gone from generational welfare to six figures and has a passion for helping women ignite their personal power and release their story of victimhood.

LaTalya is no stranger to thriving through adversity. In a five-year period, she divorced, lost her mom to lupus, and was diagnosed with a rare and highly aggressive inflammatory breast cancer.

Despite all of it, she is here today, thriving, sharing her story, and inspiring others to ignite and live a full life. During her fight with breast cancer, she self-published her first book "IGNITE: A Single Mother's Guide to Success, Sensuality and Achieving Your Dreams" and continues to nurture and love on her 4 children.

Instagram: https://www.instagram.com/coachlatalya/
Facebook: https://www.facebook.com/LifeDesignCoach
LinkedIn: https://www.linkedin.com/in/coachlatalya/

Tanya D. Powell

Dare to Thrive Through It All, Not Just Survive!

By Tanya D. Powell

"Life isn't about waiting for the storm to pass. It's about learning how to dance in the rain."
Vivian Greene

In the face of a challenge, we often ask ourselves, " Why is this happening to me?"

What if there was a more powerful question that would allow us to flow with life and thrive through all circumstances?

Most of us will face moments when our backs are against the wall. It is in those moments that we have to decide who we will be and what it is that we truly want. Do you want to struggle through the ebbs of life, or do you want to truly flow and thrive? There is a universal law called the Law of Rhythm, which states that everything goes through cycles, and everything has a rhythm or a pattern. This means that as sure as the tide goes out, it will come in. As sure as you will have good days, you will have bad ones. Are you willing to crush mediocrity?

You are probably asking, " Well, how does one rise time and time again, and do that? How does one flow despite adversity? It took some painful ebbs of life for me to understand . As a family, we built a recipe that empowered us to thrive through adversity, to be resilient, and to crush mediocrity.

"My strength lies solely in my tenacity."
Louis Pasteur

In June of 2018, my family was hit yet again with another ebb ! It had been two years of trauma and death on both sides of the family. This time, our mom was diagnosed with a life-threatening illness: colon cancer.

We were devastated, but we immediately sprang into action and met with the best doctors we could find. They informed us that given the location of her tumor, she would most likely wear a colostomy bag for the rest of her life. While we were grateful that she was okay, we knew that she wanted to thrive and live her best life.

We found a specialist in Los Angeles, California, 2,732 miles from home!

You have to be tenacious from the get-go! If you have a dream, and you want to live your best life, full of great relationships, time, and financial freedom and abundance, you have to be tenacious about it. It's your life. You can't wait for someone else to dictate it.

I quit my job without hesitation so that I could remain with my mom as her caregiver. We crashed with mom's sister and her sons. They happily gave up their space and beds. They took us to every doctor's appointment. They gave us so much love.

Your support is key. Surround yourself with the right people (and maybe it's not family). People who will support, guide, mentor and cheer you on. No man is an island. Your support ecosystem is critical.

"It's not whether you get knocked down, it's whether you get up."
Vince Lombardi.

161

The stay was an unexpected eight months long, but it turned out to be one of the best learning experiences I've had . Of course, at that time I didn't know why. Two months after returning home, I was prepared to resume my life. I had it all planned, but as if on cue, a few weeks after my birthday, I was diagnosed with breast cancer.

I had always considered myself stronger than the pack. In fact, I've been called the 'woman alpha' many times. Strong was my middle name, but in that moment I could feel my own physical strength start to slip away. As I sank to the ground in tears, I felt a strange surge of calm in my spirit.

In that moment, I made the choice to lift my eyes and focus on the breakthrough, not the breakdown, because I already knew that where my mind went, my body followed. Strength doesn't come from one's physical capacity. It comes from an indomitable spirit.

I pulled out the recipe, and as my tears gave way to laughter, I decided to grow through it, not just go through it. I bounced up immediately. My team closed ranks around me, my partner, my sister, my brother, and my mother. I thrived. Resilience is not just about bouncing back, but thriving to be your best.

Here is a quick summary of our recipe:

Tool #1 – Choice. Decide on the outcome you want. Fighting against and struggling through is not the answer. Let go and set your compass for the direction of the specific outcome you want.

Tool #2 - Perspective. Seek to reframe the situation. Find the seed of good even when it appears there is none. Our words have power, speak life, speak love, speak abundance.

Tool #3 – Mindset. Create a daily routine to strengthen your mind and keep you in unwavering faith. Where your attention goes, your energy flows.

When the ebbs of life come your way as you chase your dreams, know that life is not happening to you but with and through you, so you must let go and flow so you can truly enjoy the journey.

Remember, to thrive is to progress towards your dream in spite of!

As you read this introduction to my story, no matter what your adversity is- whether it's a broken marriage, a cancer diagnosis, or job loss, I know there is a recipe to help you thrive in the face of adversity, and you are more than equipped to crush any mediocrity or challenge. You have a power within you that is greater than that circumstance. Your indomitable spirit will allow you to rise and chase your dreams.

"You may encounter many defeats, but you must not be defeated..."
Maya Angelou

Connect with me on IG @tanyapowell1 or Tanya D Powell on FB for more about this powerful recipe and toolkit. Let's THRIVE!

Bio:
Tanya is a results coach with certifications from John Maxwell Leadership and The Capp Institute, and a former Business Coach with ActionCOACH. Tanya spent over 20 years in the financial sector, culminating in senior leader positions at multi billion dollar companies.

Despite a global pandemic and a cancer diagnosis in 2020, Tanya has emerged as a cancer thriver, and founded the ishift Institute for Transformation where she works with individuals to create a mindset shift that moves them from where they are today to where they truly long to be.

Given a new outlook on life, Tanya believes that one should seek to thrive even through adversities by focusing on the breakthroughs, not the breakdowns. Her simple message is to live a life of purpose and freedom now rather than later.

Described as passionate and a game-changer, Tanya believes that "It is in change that you discover your purpose."

Debbie T. Proctor-Caldwell

Who's Gonna Check Me? - Inside the "Boy's Club"

By Debbie T. Proctor-Caldwell

In 2015, after 25 years, I retired from a federal law enforcement agency called the United States Capitol Police (USCP) as a Lieutenant. The USCP was established in 1828, and I am the first and only Native American, female lieutenant in the history of the USCP. It wasn't until 2004 that minority females were even promoted beyond the rank of sergeant. I was promoted to sergeant in 1999 and to Lieutenant in 2006. I can assure you, this was not an easy task. The fact that minority women weren't promoted sooner definitely was not a reflection of their inability to get promoted. Most were simply tired of the harassment that came with "not knowing their place," and "trying to do a man's job," or so they were told. While others were simply tired of fighting or giving more of themselves without appreciation or acknowledgement of the great work that they had already done. Therefore, a lot of women accepted complacency.

Oftentimes throughout my career, in order to stay sane, I had to hold on tight to the Bible verse, 1 Corinthians 10:13, "… God is faithful, who will not allow you to be tempted beyond what you are able …"

I often reminded myself of the shoulders I stood on whenever I felt defeated and continued to tell myself that the trials and tribulations I was experiencing were hurdles in the race called "Life."

During the first ten years at USCP, I felt like whenever I applied for a position, I was either roadblocked, given excuses, or felt that the interviewer was just going through the motions. Instead of giving in to my frustrations and becoming complacent, I decided to be honest with myself, own up to my faults, and start with what I could control - me! I realized I needed a seat at the table of the proverbial "Boy's Club" to do so! However, in order to do that, I needed a plan. I began to picture myself in that new position. I pictured myself getting my college degrees. I pictured myself in a whole new light. I was on fire, and suddenly I was asking myself, "Who's gonna check me?"

You may think, " Pass the test, get promoted, make some changes…sounds easy, right?" That couldn't be further from the truth! Those achievements were actually just the beginning. Being a short, minority female felt like waving a banner that said , " It's okay to dismiss me!" amongst my male counterparts. However, what I learned early in law enforcement was that "knowledge," in every sense of the word, was power, and that would be my key to respect and success.

Women have to accept the fact that when they become a leader, especially in a male-dominated field, every decision they make is under scrutiny. A woman must decide whether she will be a victim to pressure from others for crumbs of acceptance, or if she is willing to withstand being ostracized today by standing on her own merit in exchange for respect tomorrow. The truth is, many cannot withstand being ostracized. However, every decision that a female leader makes, ultimately creates a path for other women to follow or makes it harder for every woman that comes after her. I kept this in mind every time I sought a promotion or position. I often said to myself, "I would be the change, directly or indirectly."

There have been many instances in my career, where I have been faced with the decision to stand up for those unable or unwilling to speak for themselves or to turn a blind eye to the wrongdoing that I witnessed. From attempts by my supervisor to coerce me into changing the outcome of a discrimination allegation by flaunting his rank to allowing another peer to continue to belittle an employee to turning a blind eye to wrongdoing, I'm proud to say I have always chosen to do the right thing and beyond. In the end, I wanted to be one of the women that crushed mediocrity and pushed those around her to excel beyond their wildest imagination. I never took it for granted, I knew that I was mentoring others with my actions, and that I was always being observed. You can only make excuses for doing nothing for so long , then it becomes a part of who you are, especially in a supervisory position. You are held to a higher standard. People have failed their families by choosing to do wrong to avoid being "black marked." Being "black marked" meant you were a difficult employee and not a team player, and that term was often a career killer.

I have learned throughout my career in law enforcement that you can either be successful or remain comfortable, but you cannot do both. In order to be successful, stop dwelling in the past, and become a woman that crushes mediocracy, you must prepare your future for success by:

1. Ask for feedback

    • Listen with an open mind

    • Research the advice given and needed improvements.

2. Make a plan

    • Accept and acknowledge your faults in how you prepared for a new position/promotion in the past.

    • Invest in yourself- Seek and attend training classes geared toward new positions/promotions.

3. Execute the plan

    • Become proficient- practice solo/groups and videotape sessions to review later.

    • Abandon comfort zone.

- o Volunteer for unfamiliar projects to gain experience.

- o Volunteer as a reviewer for position/promotion processes of other Agencies/Departments to learn the "insider" tips.

- Mentor

  - o Train others on the process

  - o Reach one, Teach One!

- Remain ethical

  - o Never allow others to compromise yourself

  - o Do a "gut check" to ensure that it is really the right thing to do.

Bio:

Debbie Proctor-Caldwell is a wife, mother of two adult children, and stepmother to her bonus son. She is from Southern Maryland but currently lives in Washington D.C. In 2015, she retired as a police lieutenant from the United States Capitol Police in Washington D.C. with over 25 years of experience in law enforcement, investigations, and public speaking. She is now an aspiring author and International, motivational speaker. Debbie is a child of God and attends the First Baptist Church of Glen Arden of Maryland. She earned her Bachelor's and Master's of Science in Management from Johns Hopkins University in Baltimore, Maryland. Debbie is currently in the process of building her business that will serve to empower Women in leadership positions with the tools needed to have their voices heard and to become successful leaders.

Email: TerenaCspeaks@gmail.com
Instagram: TerenaCspeaks@instagram.com
LinkedIn: Debbie Proctor-Caldwell, M.S.

Dr. Kenya Rawls

Night Vision; Remaining Focused in Dark Times

By Dr. Kenya Rawls

I grew up in the projects of a small town in Alabama with a population of less than 2,000 people. As a little girl, I was raised in church. I enjoyed playing with marbles, digging in the dirt, and shooting basketball. To say I was a tomboy would be an understatement. Living in a small town was great because everyone knew each other and/or was family, but it came with its challenges as well. I was taught at a very early age that what happens in the family stays in the family. I dreamt of escaping the small town and the shame of some of the secrets that were tormenting me. I didn't know how I could do it, but I figured the opportunity would come from my love for learning.

However, I didn't take my education seriously until my junior year of high school. I wanted to attend college, but in my mind I had time to "get it together." I didn't apply to college until after I graduated high school. After all, I was just a teenager. The anxiousness of waiting to hear back from schools was overwhelming. I gave myself a pep talk. I vowed to never procrastinate on making major life decisions again. To my surprise, I was accepted into a college five hours away from home. I was ecstatic to be in a "big" city and attending a University, but in reality, I also felt like I was in way over my head.

I prayed to God for guidance and strength, but every day this contended with my thoughts. I was talking myself out of accomplishing something historic by completing a degree at a HBCU.

My actions started to align with my thoughts, and I went to some of my classes and studied sporadically, but I didn't give everything necessary to succeed in school. I convinced myself again that I had time to figure it all out. The further I got behind in my coursework, the more inferior I felt to my classmates. I was trapped in a perpetual mental cycle of a cat and mouse game. I subconsciously created a culture of uncertainty in my mind by feeling I couldn't be productive in an environment I didn't belong in.

I needed a way to numb myself. I started drinking uncontrollably. Before I left for college, I was already sneaking and drinking. Before I knew it, I was an alcoholic. I was desperately trying to find my comfort zone so I could "feel" normal. I didn't want to go home, but I wasn't doing well in school. I began spiraling out of control. I was making one bad decision after the next. I started stripping, stopped going to class entirely, and eventually dropped out of school. I gave up on my dreams, and I gave up on myself. I was a failure, completely lost and unsure what to do with my life. I started to question my worth and purpose. I was extremely disappointed that I allowed myself to get to such a low place.

I didn't want to waste any more of myself living a mediocre life. I finally understood the value of time. I reached out to God, I stopped drinking, quit stripping, and wanted to go back to school. Fear was no longer a factor. God admonished me to launch out into the deep.

"God, He tells Simon to cast his nets into the deep water. Now go out where it is deeper and let down your nets to catch some fish." He replied, "we worked hard all last night and didn't catch a thing. But if you say so, I'll let the nets down again." And this time their nets were so full of fish they began to tear! A shout for help brought their partners in the other boat, and soon both boats were filled with fish and on the verge of sinking." (Luke 5:5-7)

173

With a GPA less than a 2.0, I had the audacity to apply for college again. The anxiousness of waiting to hear back from a school was still overwhelming. My pep talk this time was different. I told myself I had to tap into my faith to navigate the unknown. I wanted to fulfill my dreams. It was essential I stop living below my purpose when God created me to be above, never beneath; the head and not the tail. I accepted I had made things in my life complex, but I let Jesus simplify them. I was bogged down with the cares of the world, but Jesus said, "Cast your cares on me. I was facing some impossible battles." In Jesus, all things are possible.

I was determined not to let my past dictate my future! By a miracle, I was accepted into college again. This time I made the absolute best of the second chance I was given. I completed both my bachelor's in Psychology and master's in Human Services in three years. I earned my doctorate in Christian Counseling as well. I completed all three degrees with honors (Magna Cumm Laude). As an alcoholic little girl from a small town project, I transformed my life and rose above every obstacle by winning the battle in my mind. If you want to walk in your purpose, it's imperative to know that crushing mediocrity is a lifestyle that requires rising above your mistakes, being resilient, changing your mindset, and not wasting yourself by knowing your worth.

Bio:

Kenya Rawls was born in Dothan, Alabama. She lost her sense of purpose struggling with failure. Dr. Kenya found solace in writing poetry. This interest soon blossomed into a burning passion. She began to cultivate this interest through speaking engagements. Her gift of speaking opened doors for her to share the stage with various public figures, including the late Dr. Maya Angelou. She is also a nationally recognized poet with numerous projects. In addition to public speaking and poetry; She is a devoted wife and mother. Today her mission focuses on leading, empowering, and equipping women to discover fulfillment in living on purpose. She is the founder of S.I.S (Synergy in Sisterhood Counseling, Coaching and Consulting, LLC) Kenya believes our words have responsibility and our mind, body, spirit and soul needs to hear positivity. Follow Let's connect! Follow me on all social media platforms @ drkenyainspires

Tori Rose

The Politics of Progress: Removing "Me" from Mediocrity
By Tori Rose

Most adults who have held a corporate job, dated someone with an extremely controlling parent, or reached any level of success in leadership have used the phrase, "It's just the politics of it."

Anyone learning to navigate through these politics in the workplace or understand how to massage their mother-in-law's ego knows well what it means to approach things "politically."

There's politics in every aspect of life. People use politics to get what they want. I have learned that my growth, success, view of self, and how I ultimately matriculate through the world with my God-given gifts is also extremely political. There is a process to everything. To become who you are supposed to be in life and to leave a mark on the earth that your children can be proud of, you must learn the Politics of Progress.

While politics are often boring for some, and we may shy away from approaching life in such a calculated and strategic way all the time I ask that you indulge me for a moment and self-reflect. Let's be honest. Life has challenged us with situations that have required us to train, defend, isolate, and fight like hell! Many of us were born to be warriors of strategy!

A few years ago, I faced an epic battle against myself. I had a good job with great pay, I traveled a lot, I drove expensive cars, wore nice clothes, and lived how I wanted, but my soul was in a state of unrest. I was never truly happy. Promotion after promotion. Still not happy. Starting a new venture. Miserable. Joining a club. Bored. Dating someone new. Disenchanted. No matter what I did, in my soul, I was unhappy.

I felt out of order. I had progress with no real productivity. I had a position with no real purpose.

I set out on a journey to understand myself better. I prayed to God for clarity. One night, I heard God say, "Tori, you haven't learned the politics of progress. You haven't learned how to win. You don't know the rules of the game!"

Whoa God! That's deep.

To break the cycle of mediocrity, I needed to challenge myself to do something different. My perspective had to change! I would have to become politically savvy.

Progress doesn't happen magically! It is no different than running for office, moving to a new state, starting a new job, or starting a business: the first step of progression is having a plan. Remember, "when you fail to plan, you plan to fail." Before you attempt to do something big, you must plan it out! With planning comes learning. You need to immerse yourself in learning all you can about the thing you want to master. You must train yourself to write it out, label the steps, align it with your calendar, and have alternative plans. Planning invites order into your world, because you are inviting in God and His infinite wisdom and grace.

Successful planning breeds patience.

The next step in mastering the politics of progress is patience and removing the "ME" from Mediocrity. Patience is truly hard because you must allow vulnerability into your life to the point of discomfort. You must be willing to wait to measure the success of the actions you've implemented in your plan. You will be forced to see your weaknesses and frailties. You will feel exposed and lacking control. This is a good thing! We can take it even further, and say this is a God thing! The Bible mentions patience seventy times. God places an emphasis on patience because it is a key to progressing politically and strategically. You must master when to move, how to move, and who to take along with you.

You may be asking, "Will planning and patience propel me into purpose?" While you may begin to progress with the mastery of these two, they are not the end-all, be-all. You also must practice! If you want to become the top realtor in your area, or a best-selling author, an amazing coach, a skilled doctor, the hottest baker, etc., you need to commit to practicing each and every day. Practice is the next step in progress and requires a level of discipline and commitment that sets the great apart from the good!

For me, practice is often the hardest thing to do because it requires me to stand up and fight against decades of laziness. My assumption used to be that God's grace would cover my laziness and the absurd years of conditioning in which I've told myself that because I am gifted in this "specific area," I do not have to sharpen my skills. Can you relate? What lies have you told yourself that stop you from practicing your gift daily? What parts of being mediocre bring you comfort? I must admit, I saw nothing wrong with the mediocre in me because I was afraid to be set apart. I was afraid of the position that came along with the progression. When you are progressing, God will often position you in the front or in the center. The front means others look to you as a leader, while the center means all things flow from you as a central resource. Politics! Either way, those positions are scary and may bring you a sense of unworthiness.

One must remember God is a planner as well. He knows what plans He has for you, and they are plans to help you prosper. With that in mind, you should never see yourself as unworthy of a position of progress. It is through progress that true purpose is born, and productivity is achieved! Politics is leveraging power. You will progress and tap into your own power when you approach progress politically. Win with planning, patience, practice, and progressing politically!

Bio:

Tori Rose served in the Federal Government for over a decade where she represented underserved populations of Americans. For years, she served as an instructor, mentor, a leader in HR, and technical expert.

Tori is an entrepreneur and motivational speaker. Her businesses have a focus of enhancing the community, educating entrepreneurs, and empowering others by providing them with applicable training and resources.

In 2018, after the murder of her younger cousin, Tori founded "We Read. We Lead." which empowers adults through literacy, life skills, and employment support. Tori ran for the District 7 City Council seat in the 2020 Primary election. As the only woman candidate on the ballot, Tori was able to excite women across the city and engage many of them in political conversations for the first time in their lives. Tori Rose: Mom, Mentor, Educator.

Email Tori at connect2tori@gmail.com.
Connect to her on Instagram and Facebook @ToriRoseTheConnector

Tara Russell

Mind Your Business!
By Tara Russell

The phrase "mind your business" typically has a negative connotation, but when you are a business owner, this is the most important part of sustaining your business. How often do you feel a burning gut feeling that you should be doing more? How often do you feel an internal pull or tug that you need to do more in life? When you talk, do people listen? Do people follow you even when you are not trying to lead, but life gets in the way, your nine to five gets in the way, family emergencies, best friend drama,, and everything in between gets in your way.

I used to work for a company in the property management field, a field I love. I was born and bred for the property management field. I loved my staff, l loved my residents, and I loved the work that I did. However, I did not love the feeling of being underappreciated and undervalued. There were times when I worked 12 to 15 hour days, ordered dinner for delivery to my house so my children did not have to wait for dinner. I left work stressed, tired, and sometimes in tears because I was so unhappy. I worked for a system that believed they knew everything, and the staff was only there to push buttons, follow orders, and do work. Our opinion, past knowledge, and experience meant nothing to them. It was frustrating to sit by and watch them implement systems and processes that I knew were going to fail. I reached my five year anniversary with this company. During my five years there, I had set records, won awards, and got acknowledged twice by the president of the company for my accomplishments . During my luncheon, my supervisor made a speech. The speech was less than a minute long. Not because she did not have things to reference, but because she didn't care enough to do research about my accomplishments with this company. At that moment, it hit me that they really didn't care if I stayed or left, if I was happy or not. Part of me stayed because I felt the "job" needed me, the "residents" needed me, my "staff" needed me because no one was going to give them the same time and attention, especially because I knew how upper management felt about the residents and staff.

I chose to stay to make sure everyone was okay, and in the meantime, I passed on business opportunities, I watched others exceed and pass me by, I got distracted, and my business, my dreams, and my goals all suffered. I had that gut-wrenching, burning feeling in my stomach. I had that internal pull and tug saying, "You need to do more for you." I had a decision to make, and after being disappointed time and time again with this company I decided to leave. I did not fully know how to go about this, but I knew something had to change fast. I refused to continue living the cycle of work, stress, and repeat.

I started to mind my business! I made changes in my professional career to allow myself to mind my business. For example, instead of working through my lunch, I used my lunch hour to do work for my clients. Instead of working 12 hour days, I made a conscious decision to leave on time so I could get home to my family and my clients. I started to give all the extra I gave my employer to myself. In changing how I approached my employer, I gave myself permission to do what I needed to do for me and my family, and you can do the same!

- Do not get distracted by things being thrown at you, not even your job.

- Have the courage to step down from your stability to step up to your greatness.

- Have the courage to walk away from what you think is your safety net to achieve your goals. Sometimes your safety net

185

will hold you back and not allow you the freedom to do what burns in your heart to do.

- Become a beast with your time and your intention.

Now, let's fully understand how to mind our business as an entrepreneur. Are you a start-up? Have an idea and not sure where to start? Here is a few tips to help get you started and make sure your back office business is in check:

1. Determine viability.

2. Create a business plan.

3. Figure out the money.

4. Choose a business name and register a domain name.

5. Incorporate / figure out legal structure and Apply for an EIN.

Are you a seasoned business owner who needs to mind your business? Here are a few tips to assist with your front office business:

1. Be Intentional with your marketing.

2. Understand your audience and be extremely clear on your niche.

3. Conduct market research and know the leaders in your industry.

4. Do daily income producing activity.

5. Have a lead generating arsenal.

Know that you are a force to be reckoned with. You are a doer, an earth-shaking mountain-mover. Step into your greatness with power, intention, and purpose. I specialize in helping businesses make a name in the midst of the noise. I'd love to stay connected with you and help you take advantage of my free resources. Connect with me at

TRUCreatiiveConsulting.com and TRU Creative Consulting on all social platforms.

Bio:

Serial entrepreneur who believes in multiple streams of income. Tara considers herself a 'Jane of All Trades and Master of Many.' Tara is the Founder and CEO of TRU Creative Consulting, TRU Properties, Co-Founder of Evolve & Empower, Chair Woman of Black Wall Street Global, Co-Host of 3 The Hardway Talk Show. Tara is a marketing and business strategist who specializes in helping businesses make a name in the midst of the noise.

Stay connected at:
www.TRUCreativeConsulting.com,
Facebook, Instagram, Tik Tok and Linkedin: TRU Creative Consulting.

WOMEN CRUSHING MEDIOCRITY

Diana Smith

Loveless at First Site
By Diana Smith

Two years after my failed marriage, I met the man of my dreams through a dating site. This was risky, but spontaneous, even for me at the time. "What is the worst that could happen?" I thought to myself. The following Friday night, I met Tony at a restaurant local to both of us in Virginia. As we greeted one another, Tony told me, "Your online profile doesn't do you no justice, you're even more attractive in person." I stood there smiling ear to ear. Things went well, and Tony and I hit it off. One date led to another, and before I knew it, things were getting serious. I introduced him to my pride and joy, my daughters, Ashley, BJ, and CeCe. We were like a family; he would pick us up for church every Sunday, then stop in D.C. to sit with his parents before heading home.

Everything was fine on the surface, but I noticed Tony was controlling. I never thought to question it. Instead, I ignored the red flags. Besides, he said he loved me. Over a year later, one Saturday night, I called him like always before going to bed to say good night, but to my surprise, Tony did not pick up his phone. I left a message. Feeling like something was wrong, I got up, got dressed, and peaked in on my girls who were sleeping before I rushed out the door.

As I was driving, I kept calling him. The calls went straight to voicemail. I became frustrated. It was not like him to ignore my calls. As I approached his apartment complex, I became triggered with thoughts of Tony cheating on me. I desperately wanted to know who was in the apartment with him. I wondered, and as my suspicion grew, so did my blood pressure.

I banged on his door so loud that I am certain the whole neighborhood heard me acting like a mad woman. After getting no response, I drove home with tears streaming down my face. I felt hurt, embarrassed, and ashamed.

The next morning was normal. I made breakfast for my daughters, then we headed to church. During the drive home from Sunday service, I received a call from Tony. He acted as if nothing happened the night before, and in a calm and stern voice, I asked, "Where were you last night?" He responded, "I turned my phone off to get some sleep." I rolled my eyes and thought, 'He must think I am stupid.' I responded, "OK!" "See you tonight" he replied, before hanging up. Tony arrived that evening with gifts. I remembered an older woman telling me that if a man shows up with gifts after being away with no explanation, they are called "guilt gifts." He acted as though he came to save the day. I played nice. I smiled and thanked him. It got late, and with the girls in the bed, Tony and I retreated to my bedroom.

Nothing could have prepared me for what happened next. As Tony walked towards the closet, his phone, which was laying on the arm of the sofa where I sat, started ringing very loud. I never understood why he kept the volume so high, but without thinking anything of it, I glanced down. Tony had received a naked picture of a woman, standing in front of his dresser with a text that said, " Thank you for a great time last night." I was livid to say the least. Tony asked me to calm down and suggested we go for a drive and talk about what happened. I agreed so I wouldn't wake my daughters and without warning, Tony pulled the car over, and he retrieved a gun from underneath his seat and threatened my life. He said, "The girls won't have a mother if you keep talking..." At that moment, everything went black. I found myself in a dark place. How did I get here? Instead of giving into fear, I looked him in the eye with his gun pointed in my face, and with composure, said, " Go ahead, but you're coming with me."

As Tony drove back towards my home, I was filled with emotions. I was suffocating as I sat next to him, counting down the minutes until I could get as far away from him as possible. On my way out the car, he yelled, "You have nothing going for yourself but a pretty face and nice breasts." I had nothing else to say. I slammed the door and walked away. I knew that would be the last time I saw him. I held it together long enough to reach my bedroom, where I kneeled to the floor and wept like a baby, crying out to God for a way to escape, not only from that relationship, but from the perpetual state of illusion of what I Psalms thought love was. I found myself, again, heartbroken and full of pain.

That day was my awakening.

147:3 says "He heals the brokenhearted and binds up their wounds."

I realized that for a long time, I had an obscured view of love, but deep down, I knew it was not supposed to feel like it did. The lesson that having sex does not equal love was a painful lesson to learn. For if we do not know our own self-worth, no one else will either.

On August 17, 2010, my family and I relocated from Virginia to Maryland, and we became members of our new church, where I began my transformative self-love journey serving in the women's ministry and sharing my story to women struggling to get out of domestic, abusive relationships. I continue to inspire women to love who they are with no apologies through my podcast, Love is Grace.

God turned my pain into purpose.

Romans 8:28, "And we know that all things work together for good to those who love God, to those who are called according to His purpose".

Bio:
Diana is a Certified Life Coach, Speaker, Founder, and Host of the Love is Grace Podcast. She stands on a strong foundation of faith. While serving in ministry, she birthed her passion to inspire and motivate women to be relentless in their pursuit of self-discovery, self-love, and personal growth. Diana spent years journaling about her bout with thyroid cancer and domestic abuse. She now shares her story to promote healing with actionable steps to release toxic patterns and unapologetically become the best version of yourself. Diana is a native of New Jersey, but resides in Maryland. She is a proud mom of three, beautiful adult daughters: Ashley, BJ, and CeCe and enjoys spending time with her grandson, Cameron.

Podcast: anchor.fm/loveisgrace.com
Website: dianasmith.co
Connect with me: Instagram & Facebook: @iamjusdiana

Deneen Swann

Until God Alone Is Enough
By Deneen Swann

Despair! Emptiness! That was all I could feel. There was nothing left. Nothing to give, nothing to hope for, nothing to live for. No husband, no home, no money, no business, Nothing! That was my life in Fall of 2014. I remember that moment like it was yesterday. It was my bottom, and I had never been there before. Everything I had built my life around was gone.

Reality Check! It was a crisp, fall evening in 2014 when I attended a financial planning seminar. These guys had been calling me for weeks, so as an understanding salesperson, I obliged the appointment. After all, everyone should be in the know about their finances and money, especially if they are starting over as a single person. I needed to know what financial moves to make at that point in my life. We set the appointment, and he assured me that the meeting would only take an hour. When I arrived at the meeting, there were five other people there. The setting was a small conference room with a small enough crowd to get our questions answered. We sat there totally engaged as the gentleman detailed a masterful, financial plan for our lives. You know the stuff= Saving for retirement, your children's college funds, purchasing a home, etc. I was so excited at the end of the presentation, I said to myself, "I can do this!" He finished the presentation by telling us that we could start an amazing wealth journey with a small investment of $500.00. It hit me: Where would I get $500.00? I ran through all my possible resources, and there were none! My heart started beating fast, and it pained me to take a breath. I realized I was holding back the tears of an emotional breakdown. My eyes teared up

196

more and more as he explained how affordable this plan was to start. When I could not take it anymore, I excused myself and left the meeting. I walked to my car as fast as I could, and when I got in, I put my head down on the steering wheel and let out a cry that stifled me. There was no sound coming out of my mouth even though it was wide open. All I could feel was tension in my face and tears flowing. That was the moment that I realized I was broke.

The Shift! In 2012, my life took a catastrophic turn. My marriage of over 20 years was over. I moved out of my 7,800 square foot dream home into a 600 square foot apartment. The master bedroom at my former house was bigger than my entire apartment. My biological father died in October of 2012. My daddy, who raised me, died in November of 2012, and my business was lackluster to say the least.

A profoundly interesting aspect of life is that most of us believe that bad things happen suddenly, but when we really sit back and think about it, there was always a slow deterioration of whatever has fallen apart. Most of us sit in a bubble while everything comes apart because we are caught up in the business of life and what seems important in the moment while the termites of life are eating away at our foundation until, one day, the floor drops from under us leaving nothing but a pile of dust.

Decision! I spent at least an hour in that car feeling sorry for myself and wondering what my life was going to be like. I was 50 years old at that point. The last thing I wanted to do was start over. I must have been crazy to make the decisions I made two years ago. What the hell was I thinking? These were the thoughts that went through my mind. I felt hopeless, and in the middle of all those thoughts, a still-small voice came to me. "Your latter days will be greater than your former days," and just like that, I remembered who I was and whose I was. I lifted my head from that steering wheel and, as I drove home, I began to thank God for giving me the strength to be brave enough to make the decisions I made. I praised him for keeping me during that time and bringing me to this place of awareness. I decided that night that I would allow God to guide me in everything I did. You see, He already was. I just wasn't aware. I accepted Jesus Christ as my Lord and Savior as a child, but in my early 40's, I surrendered my life to Christ and asked that His will be done rather than my own. I wanted His best for me, and I knew he could handle this better than me. I realized that night my life would never be the same.

My Spiritual Awakening! I wish I could state that things instantly got better, but they did not. In fact, they seemed to get progressively worse. Making a big turn in life is like steering a huge ship. The captain turns the wheel slowly, and the ship makes a series of pivots until it's going in the right direction. That's what re-building is when you do it God's way. What I learned in that time between Fall of 2014 and now is that if I wanted an amazing life full of joy, peace, and prosperity, I had to sell all-out to God. I had lonely times, a lot of crying times, some almost-getting=evicted times, food stamp times, and everything in between. I learned to receive God's gifts and blessings, which is difficult as a giver. I stopped trying to fix everything on my own and learned to trust GOD completely for every detail of my life. I learned that God and I alone were enough.

Bio:
Deneen Swann is a Real Estate Broker licensed in Washington D.C., Maryland, and Virginia. She is a Top Producing Agent at KW Metro Center in Tysons Corner with over 20 years of experience. She specializes in helping families list, market, sell, and purchase homes. Her approach to serving her clients is to first understand what their needs and goals are, and create a personalized plan that will accomplish those goals. This approach is what led Deneen to her motto: "It's not about the house, it's about the family that lives there."

Deneen is also the owner and operator of Realty Solutions Unlimited, a property management and real estate solutions company. She is a member of the Northern Virginia Association of Realtors Top

Producers Club and the Agent Leadership Counsel at KW Metro Center. Deneen also coaches and mentors new real estate agents, as well as women struggling to find themselves after divorce.

Kim M. Swann

Falling for Me. Story of Faith, Hope and Love
By Kim M. Swann

The year of 2012, I was reborn. Not biblically, but in the sense of being free.

My daddy, my lifeline and one of my best friends recently passed from a debilitating disease known as Alzheimer's. Rewind to 2005. My father was diagnosed with this horrific disease, which I remember vividly as if it was only the other day. During his early months of the illness, we visited Johns Hopkins to see a Dementia specialist. While waiting in the examination room, my father instructed me on what my next steps in life should be. He told me that I should maintain a well paying job, lose some weight, and continue to raise my daughter both financially and emotionally. Such intense conversations were typical of our relationship. Even after his death, I welcomed his presence around me. While sitting next to my father as he began to understand this information, I noticed the expression on his face and movement throughout his body. He gladly stood and said, "Is that all, Let's go Kim." As we were walking to the car, my father, being himself, greeted everyone passing us by on the way to the car. Once we got in the car, he said to me, "Well, I guess I will have to fight this one too." Which meant Alzheimer's was not going to win.

In life, there are events that create pivotal and thoughtful shifts. That statement by my father shifted my life, at least for that moment, that day, and that time. The world as I knew it stopped and did not move again until I felt it all within me. It shifted my feelings, my spirit, and my soul. As I moved forward, my thoughts on what my life could be, should be, or would be changed constantly. Every day, I woke up in the middle of the night wondering why I was where I was in life. I was in a marriage that was immersed in infidelity and abuse. I was a mom to a busy teenager who struggled with the notion that my father's days on this side of heaven were numbered. My thoughts shifted between how I would feel once my father transitioned and where I should be in life. These thoughts became mental struggles that played over and over in my head. Don't get it twisted, I still conducted myself accordingly as a wife and mother, but I knew that suffering from pre-mourning was settling in as well. My reality shifted my perspective, and for that I am forever grateful.

My dad's consistent reminder to keep my good job played like the tune of a national anthem in my head, but I knew that I wanted more in life, more in love, and more of myself. I knew that I was in a marriage of convenience, but not my final destination. The questions remained. How do I escape my inner thoughts that keep haunting me? How do I find my freedom? How do I live on without my father, my Daddy? What is my next destiny or chapter? How do I keep the faith, hope, and love?

From these questions, I learned to seek God's wisdom and guidance in my next steps. I prayed over and over for a simple sign or answer. I asked "Are you guiding me on the right path to my victory?" I did not feel complete. I did not feel whole. As time passed by, I witnessed the ugly truth of Alzheimer's disease. How did a single diagnosis, single conversation eventually kidnap my father? The only person who I felt held me accountable and made me feel complete was now processing his own death. My dad's illness became more present. Reality started showing up. I knew that one day soon, my dad would not even know who I am.

Dealing with a parent slowly losing the battle to this horrific disease is the most unfair emotion to deal with. On top of that, you're expected to conduct life as we know.

Let me be clear. I am a mother; a mother to a daughter who had a full schedule with school, weekend, and church priorities. In fact, my daughter was taking two ice skating classes, singing with two elite national performance choirs , and actively participating in our church dance ministry. To say the least, she was a world traveler before her senior year. Oh, I forgot, she was also a high school debutante. Basically, my life was her life. I poured every inch of my life and time into my daughter. She became my morning, afternoon, and night. This is what moms do, right? We halt our dreams, and put our vision on pause. Does this sound familiar?

Fast Forward. My father began to actively transition. The idea of my last time seeing my father squeeze my hands was an ever-present reality. My prayers didn't stop. My thoughts at night still kept me awake. My visions of personal freedoms were extremely present in my mind, but I had to stay focused, keep smiling, and keep saying to all, "I am good." In fact, I had to keep the faith, hope, and love.

Next. Daddy sighed his last breath. His physical being was gone, but his presence was stronger than ever. His voice became even louder in my head as If he saw the real me.

The shift started to occur. During the week of planning my father's funeral , I discovered my then husband had an affair and impregnated the woman. I intentionally left him out of the obituary in the local newspaper to do my father more justice. Divorce was imminent.

My father eventually transitioned. I became divorced. My daughter graduated from high school and all those priorities were diminished. I asked, "Has God allowed me to see the road that was once blocked and opened the path for me?" I left my job of 15 years, started a new company, moved to a new city, and purchased my new home in cash. It was time for me to lean into my shift. For years, I devoured myself in my marriage and family, but all the while I was losing myself.

God spoke, my dad's voice was clear, and I knew that it was time to free myself. Finally, I was crushing in business, in life, and in myself. I was in the shift-and-pivot phase. I was finally free and falling for myself.

Bio:
With over 20 years of experience in corporate/non-profit/political fundraising/campaign strategy for the medical community, NGO's governmental and consulting field, she shares a deep dedication to the philanthropic communities throughout the world. Kim is the Principal of Kimetics Solutions LLC. Kim's executive interests and experience have allowed her to serve on the committee for the Mandela Washington Fellowship for Young African Leaders as advisor and participant for President Barack Obama's 2014 U. S. Africa Leader Summit. She is the founder of the Women's Platform and a member of the Baltimore City Women's Commission. Kim is a mother of one daughter and mentor to many others.

Instagram: Kimetics_1
Twitter: Kimetics
Email: Kimeticssolutions@gmail.com

Michelle S. Thomas

What Will Your Legacy Be?
By Michelle S. Thomas

Throughout history, women have experienced unbalanced opportunities for power, and even when they achieve powerful positions, still find themselves fighting for the same level of respect as their male counterparts.

Mainstream business practices throughout time remain heavily structured with "male friendly" policies and principles. Many of us have seen certain businesses promote women "initiatives" strictly for publicity rather than implementing real change. . Even in 2021, there are still women working in certain industries and positions that must choose between their family, children, and rise to success. Many young ladies are looking for positive examples of strong women that are crushing their business success while still proud to embrace their womanhood. Make today the day that we stop compromising, contorting, and conceding to business models not designed to empower us. Change the narrative, not only locally, but globally and become " unapologetic" for the powerful woman you were designed to be!

We stand at a pivotal point for our future, and together, we can shift the pendulum permanently into a firmer level of equality. We are setting precedents that are landing us into our best position to elevate. We have the first black female vice president, racial targeting by law enforcements being exposed, states breaking 30-year voting traditions, and professional sports leagues taking a financial and public stand. We are seeing solidarity movements that positively resemble the movements of the past gain support around the world. Movements that forever revolutionized rights for humankind. A new generation is ready to stand together for change. What will your legacy be?

Know that you are the only one who can do what you do. Embrace who you are as a woman, and accentuate what you bring to the business world. You have skills, trends, and knowledge that can present the perfect solution for someone else's problem . We must stop diminishing our qualities to fit into the small box history has set aside for us. Break those barriers open, and show the world how great you are! Together, we have the ability to change antiquated methods of thinking, believing, and operating. The best way for us to do this is to all empower each other. We must shed our fear of standing out, standing up, and standing strong. As you build your business or grow your career, strive to find the impact you can make for yourself, our daughters, and future power-destined women. There are many ways that we can empower each other, however, our largest platforms of impact will need to be within our social, educational, economic, political, and psychological environments. No matter the size of your business, you can have an impact. Yes, I get it, running a business is hard, however, there are very simple things we can do as women that will have a lasting impact on the ladies following in our footsteps. Let's explore some suggestions that you can initiate, whether you are a business owner or business supporter.

Social Empowerment

Can your business promote empowerment via its social image? Unlike our ancestral women before us, we have the instant ability to make transformations globally . Stand up for women's equality publicly, stand out by supporting your sister businesses, and stand strong by volunteering for your local women's shelter, domestic abuse organizations, or women and children advocacy groups.

Educational Empowerment

Are you sharing tips and tools with other young, female entrepreneurs? Yes, you are in business to be profitable, so giving away all your trade secrets for free may not be the goal. However, you can run a training clinic once a year for economically disadvantaged young ladies or offer to speak at a local school, and tell your story. This may completely change the outlook of a young lady that may not have positive examples of women in her life. Your story, path, and experiences will be far more educational than reading someone else's who they may never meet.

Economic Empowerment

Were you aware that small businesses contribute to over 44 percent of the U.S. economy? There are economic opportunities you can offer that will not break your finances. As a sole proprietor, you can build into your budget to offer an annual, two-week paid internship to a young woman interested in your industry. If you have a larger business, ensure that you promote equal pay, opportunities, and benefits to the women you employ. Offer flex time to your employees to lessen the stressors mothers bear when working with children.

Political Empowerment

Did you know that businesses carry more political influence than individuals? Stay involved with the changes happening within your community and beyond. Join your local and state chamber of commerce. Recognize what your current political leaders are doing for businesses of all sizes and hold them accountable for the platforms they run on. Strengthen your knowledge about the political impacts affecting women, your community, and minorities.

Psychological Empowerment

This is where you can have your broadest impact. In the words of International Speaker and Author, Dr. Cheryl Woods, "You have the prescription for someone else's pain!" Your presence, encouragement,

210

and time can turn someone's life around. Walk in your power! Let's stop judging, minimizing, and stepping on each other, and increase our uplifting, encouraging, and empowering of one another . First, become active in your own psychological empowerment. Understand your value in everything that you do. Establish meaning within all tasks no matter how large or small. Exercise self-motivation to push yourself through distractions. Build your own mission, vision, and values, and apply them to everything you are involved in. Start with yourself to strengthen your ability to lead by example. Show others how to believe in themselves, take ownership of their destiny. and elevate above discouragement. Consider that no one has ever told them that they are great, important, and empowered. Start your legacy and make yourself their first !

Bio:

Michelle S. Thomas, Your Relationship Surgeon is an International Best-selling Author, Certified Life, Relationship, and Business Coach, Motivational speaker, and multiple business owner. She believes that everyone has the power to "touch" their dreams. Even before she turned her purpose into her profession, she always recognized that real people needed to hear real stories to conquer what mattered to them. Her own life story has at times, been one of complicated paths, but she has never shied away from telling her truth. Through her own transparency, her audiences receive tools that can alleviate their pain, inspire their strength, and resurrect their inner drive. Your Relationship Surgeon offers relatable content through her books, private coaching, workshops, and keynote speeches designed to elevate your relationship with yourself, your family, and your business.

Connect today with Your Relationship Surgeon at:
Website: www.michellesthomas.com
Facebook: https://www.facebook.com/YourRelationshipSurgeon
Instagram: https://www.instagram.com/yourrelationshipsurgeon/
Twitter and Clubhouse: @YourRelaSurgeon

Tammy Shannel Thurman

Do you want change or more of the same?
By Tammy Shannel Thurman

I want to talk to those who are stuck, who are sick and tired of being sick and tired! Do you want change or more of the same? Whomever you are, you have the power to change the situation you are in. I was in that very same desolate place for many years. Waking up in the morning, only thinking about how challenging the day was going to be—going to bed thinking about how I had to do it all over again tomorrow. One day I found myself just complaining away in front of the right person at the right time. She said to me, "if you want to see change, you have to first renew your mind, renew your thinking because what you believe is exactly what you see!" Bells began ringing and I accepted what she said because it was the TRUTH!

It was time to CRUSH my mediocre way of thinking, seeing, and living. What was so amazing in the crushing process was the environment, and all it encompassed never changed. How I saw the day did! It had to start with how I believed. I had to change how I perceived for my days to change. I was reminded of a passage of scripture Jeremiah 29:11. "For I know the thoughts that I think toward you, saith the Lord, thoughts of peace, and not of evil, to give you an expected end." That passage lets me know that there is greater in store for me and where I am now is working for my good. Let me be clear; this wasn't just a one-and-done thing. This was my daily meditating on affirmations and scriptures to renew my thinking.

I started noticing a change in how I talked and how I looked and felt. I would look in the mirror and see a woman who is fearfully and wonderfully made by God. There was nothing common or ordinary about me—quite the opposite. I was created with great reverence and respect to be unique and set apart. When I tapped into that moment in time, there was no way I was ever going to turn back. Why would I? I wanted change in me and my journey. To recognize what was holding me back all that time and not do anything was more of the same and not change! Again, do you want change or more of the same? I could have gotten an attitude with the lady. After all, she didn't know my story. She wasn't living these challenging days that I was. But I was sick and tired of being sick and tired. I wanted change and not more of the same.

This crushing process took about a year for me to not only renew my mind daily but for it to stick in the right direction. To be honest, it never felt like a year because I saw so many things that I had missed out on and was now enjoying them. The process led me from ordinary expectations to extraordinary desires. I found myself smack dab in the middle of God's perfect plan, that plan to prosper me. A year later, I found myself headed to the biggest interview of my life. I found myself accepting a new career making six figures and loving it. Seven years later, I found myself being honored for outstanding leadership to the State of North Carolina, the Leadership North Carolina Board of Directors, and the Office of the Governor. Eight years later, I found myself as the executive producer of my own radio talk show and CEO of a motivational movement for females of all ages and racial backgrounds.

There is so much more to the story about how I crushed mediocrity and landed back into the will of God's plan. You can have faith, but if you don't work it, it dies. What I want you to take away is that crushing mediocrity for some will mean changing the way you believe because this will change the way you see everything.

Do you want change or more of the same? We will see!

Bio:

Tammy Thurman is a philanthropist, motivational speaker, mentor, community leader, radio talk show host, executive producer, and Woman of God. She is the founder and CEO of A Nation of Sisters. As CEO of A Nation of Sisters, she empowers, inspires, and motivates many females of all ages and colors to be the best they can be to themselves and their communities. Tammy was honored for outstanding leadership experience and dedicated service to the State of North Carolina, the Leadership North Carolina Board of Directors, and the Office of the Governor. She is a recipient of the prestigious 45 under 45 of St. Augustine's University and the prestigious North Carolina Governor's Award for Volunteer Service. She holds a Bachelor of Arts in Communication from St. Augustine's University and is a licensed minister.

To learn more about her, please visit www.anationofsisters.com

Tish Times

Crushing Mediocrity is Now a Daily Practice
By Tish Times

Crushing mediocrity is now a daily practice for me. There were, of course, a few events that pushed me to decide that I would no longer tolerate mediocrity as my comfort zone. I started my first business in 2000. It was a staffing company that took a quick, upward rise to success (as did my ego).

The year 2007 marked my twelve year wedding anniversary. My husband Roy and I were taking our first vacation ever. We planned to join each other at the end of his business meeting and stay an additional three or four days. We had a lovely vacation and were finishing up a tour of the Yucatan Peninsula when I received a very disturbing call. It was Friday- payday back at home for my employees. I had prepared everything prior to my departure, and my staff was knowledgeable enough to handle most issues. The call caused my relaxing trip to take a terrible turn. My assistant told me that she had released the payroll checks, but many employees were at the office stating that the bank wouldn't cash their checks because there was no money available. This statement baffled me because, as I mentioned, I had made sure that everything was ready to go for payroll before I left. I was thousands of miles away, and I had no idea why the bank was saying there was no money in our account when I was positive there was. After several calls to my bank, I found out that three checks from one of our clients had bounced. I was devastated. It was the same client that had defaulted on a payment of almost $20,000 several months earlier. I gave them a repayment agreement which they broke, but after

218

threats to sue, they made some payments. They agreed to make daily payments since they ran a cash business, and for a while, it worked out. Apparently, they had additional problems because the last three payments, one which was large, bounced. This caused a serious problem for my company that was compounded by the fact that the client shortly after went bankrupt. We didn't recover the money. We never recovered at all. During the process, several employees had long delays before getting paid. Due to the constant stream of angry calls and employee visits, I lost all of my staff members. The story ran on the local news twice, and although the first time I made a statement to explain the reason for the issue, my words were twisted and taken out of context so that I looked like a greedy business owner who refused to pay her employees. Our company went from hundreds of temporary employees each week to none at all. Because of the bad press and payroll problems, I lost every client I had. The issues we faced were severe and costly, but the lessons learned in the process were invaluable. Although this story may make you want to feel sympathy for me, I discovered new things about myself during this time.

I mentioned earlier that as my business grew quickly, so did my ego. I made poor decisions in an effort to keep up appearances. Instead of dealing with the client immediately and communicating intent to sue them for every dime that was owed, I was forgiving. You may ask, "What's wrong with that?" After much reflection, I realize that I wasn't being compassionate because I was concerned about that company. I allowed the guilt that I had for all of the times I didn't pay my bills or when I had 'floated' checks to color what should have been a black and white decision. My own low self-esteem got in the way of not only my success, but the success of all those connected to me. I allowed my old habit of manipulating my money to meet my immediate needs to creep back in. I used money that was allocated for something else to try to fix the problem, which made matters worse. Instead of asking someone for help, I refused to admit what I considered to be failure and allowed pride to prevent myself from reaching out to those who could have made an investment into my business or given me a loan to turn the situation around. I didn't allow my perception of myself to be replaced with how God sees me, and I reverted back to doing what I used to do instead of what was right. My desire to please people and appear successful caused me to make devastating decisions that resulted in the failure of my business.

Although I was an excellent salesperson, passionate about customer service, and competent administratively, I wasn't the best money manager. No one knew this better than me. Yet, I decided to move forward and trust that somehow God would assist me with my weaknesses, and He did. He allowed them to come to the forefront and gave me the opportunity to deal with them properly. I chose to revert to what was familiar. Through that ordeal, He helped me realize that I can only accomplish what I believe I can accomplish. I remember being in my office, saying to myself over and over again, "I don't know what I am doing!" I already believed that I was financially incompetent, so saying it over and over increased my faith in the fact that I didn't know what I was doing. My actions then began to follow that very statement.

I can finally be honest with myself. I don't hide behind any facades, and I no longer create them to impress others. This lesson from years ago helps me daily. My confidence as a sales professional is higher because I can trust myself to do what is best for my clients and make business decisions that best serve my team and my life.

Bio:

Tish Times is the founder of Tish Times Networking and Sales Training. Tish is a certified networker, community builder, and franchise owner for Network in Action in Phoenix, Arizona. For over ten years, Tish has been empowering businesses to create revenue-generating business connections, follow-up effectively, stay top-of-mind, shorten the sales cycle, and close sales with ease.

Tish and her team help skyrocket her client's revenue with a done-for-you sales solution. Tish Times is an expert at helping companies to attract more leads, maintain a full pipeline, and convert more prospects to clients.

Tish's books include Networking is Not a One-Night Stand, The Unstoppable Confidence Networking Playbook and The Networking and Sales Planner.

You can find her at www.TishTimes.com or contact her at
Email: tish@tishtimes.com
Facebook: www.facebook.com/coachtishtimes
LinkedIn: www.linkedin.com/in/tishtimes

Alethia Tucker

Conquering Complacency to Secure My Destiny
By Alethia Tucker

Somewhere along the line, we've been told that we have to focus on one thing in order to be successful. At least that's what I was told growing up. I was also told that there were certain careers that I should not pursue because "there was no money in that field." Both of my parents came from humble beginnings, and like many, were determined to ensure that I not only had the opportunity to go to college, but also make the best use of my education. So, off I went to college and pursued the things that seemed right for me. However, I had a hard time trying to find that one thing that I liked. I experimented until the last possible moment I had to declare my major. After switching my major five times and taking classes year-round, I graduated in four years, with the major I originally started, political science.

After graduation, I found myself beginning what would turn into a paralyzing cycle. Like most kids, I was told that I could be anything I wanted to be when I grew up. I could do anything! I just couldn't figure out what "anything" looked like for me. For years I went from position to position, trying to find my fit- or really just trying to find a job that seemed like a good position to have. So, the kid who could do anything she wanted to do, decided to fit the mold. What developed over a number of years made me miserable. I was going from place to place, being effective at what I did, but not really liking anything. I landed coveted internships with both federal and state governments. I went on to get wonderful jobs working in corporate America. I pursued the positions because I knew that they were great opportunities. However, many times I questioned whether or not these great opportunities were the best choice for me. Don't get me wrong, every job that I've held made substantial contributions to my family. Our needs were met, the kids were in private school, we vacationed every year, and we were able to afford many of the luxuries we desired. I will be forever grateful for the skills and knowledge that I've acquired, the projects I've worked on, the people I've managed, and the contributions I've made. However , why is it that I came home every day feeling like something was missing? Why did I frequently question the hurried life I was leading ? Why was I depressed and dealing with health issues? I needed answers.

In 2019, I heard a talk given by Elizabeth Gilbert, the author of the famous book, *Eat, Pray, Love*. During the talk, Elizabeth described two types of people. There was one group that's single- focused. She called these people "Jackhammers." She said that they knew what they wanted and furiously hammered at that one spot. Then she mentioned another group which she described as "Hummingbirds." Like the pollinators they are, the Hummingbirds move from flower to flower, leaving pollen on every spot that they visit. When I heard this description, something clicked. Was she saying that everyone didn't focus on one area when they chose a career? I spent so many years trying to make myself fit the mold of the positions I held, not because they were just right for me, but because they were good enough. Was she saying that I didn't have to be laser-focused on one particular mold in order to be successful?

This revelation took years of weight off of my shoulders. Exactly a year prior to hearing this talk, I published my first book, the *50 Things I've Learned on My Way to 50*. In the book, I share the lessons I've learned over the years leading up to my 50th birthday. Writing and publishing the book helped me realize that I wanted more out of my pursuits. Hearing Elizabeth Gilbert gave me permission to pursue more.

Some months after hearing Elizabeth's talk, I launched Jolease Enterprises, where I deliver signature coaching programs that are designed to build confidence and equip women to grab hold of the life and career that they desire. I help women to see that, whether a Jackhammer or a Hummingbird, they are exceptional and outstanding just the way they are. I share my story with women to free them from limiting beliefs that are keeping them from pursuing what they truly desire. So, what do I tell women who are trying to identify their path, trying to break out of the mold they were told to fit in, or lacking the confidence to boldly move forward?

First, realize that every experience in your journey has equipped you to make a unique imprint. Do not discount anything that you've experienced. If you look back at your journey, you will be able to find answers and pull wisdom that will further you in the direction that you desire to go. Even situations that were negative provided lessons. Second, there isn't a mold that you fit. The way you were designed is proof of this. Even identical twins aren't genetically identical. The only mold that you should feel compelled to fit is your own. Remember that, when fitting the mold, you're required to take care of all that it houses. Self-care is crucial to sustaining your vision. Finally, there is a problem somewhere that requires a one-of-a-kind answer. That problem is waiting on you. Pursue that idea that sounds impossible to do. Work on doing what fulfills you. You were designed to make a distinct mark on the world. It is crucial to embrace what you have, know that you can make a difference, and go do it.

Bio:

Alethia Tucker is an Author, Coach, and Motivational speaker who found her heart's work in helping others. She has a passion for working with women. As the visionary behind Jolease Enterprises, she works with her clients to develop the mindset, courage, and determination needed to move them from feelings of frustration and failure, to the realization of what they desire in their life and career. As a Motivational Speaker, Alethia has spoken on numerous conference and workshop platforms, encouraging and empowering her audiences. When speaking, she draws from personal experiences to encourage increased self-awareness and resilience. Her mantra is "We all have a problem that only we can solve. It is our obligation to society to find that problem and present the answer."

Dr. Nicole Valle

The Power of Vulnerability
By Dr. Nicole Valle

The power of vulnerability is very personal to me. This is the place that all my work comes together. I always thought that vulnerability was the same as weakness, andwe associate vulnerability with emotions we want to avoid such as fear, shame, and uncertainty. In a world where "never enough" dominates and feeling afraid has become second nature, vulnerability is subversive and uncomfortable. I learned it can be very dangerous at times when we put ourselves out there, which means there's a greater risk of getting hurt. As a child, I experienced family dysfunctions, and somewhere in my subconscious, I began to form emotional armor, which made me begin to shut down. I became numb and used other tactics to avoid feeling weak or vulnerable. This behavior followed into adulthood and I now know was a contributing factor in the demise of my past marriage. I didn't know how much I had sacrificed in the name of self-defense. The myths of vulnerability, the common misconceptions about weakness, which were told to me by someone else hurts trust and self-sufficiency. Over the years, I've realized that I am loyal, trustworthy, and lovable. I love hard simply for the connection that comes with love and belonging. However, if my sense of connection was off, my emotions cut people off and a vicious side of me would rise up, and I would feel nothing as if they were a perfect stranger. I never recognized what makes me shut down but then I noticed how I used perfectionism as a tactic to avoid vulnerability. Research shows how we try to ward away disappointment with a shield of cynicism. Something I learned about myself was that my biggest fear was being looked at as a fool or made to feel like a fool. For years, I believed this behavior was one of my strengths because it made me resilient through trials and tribulations. Until my now-husband came into my life and burst my bubble. After observing my behavior, he shared that it's my weakness. This is where my work begins. Needless to say, my husband is a hard teacher. He holds no punches and tells it like it is. He's a minister, so not only do I have this man straight-shooting with me, but I have the Holy Spirit working through him. I was wowed because half the stuff he said to me made me think, "How did he know that? He's just starting to get to know me!" He would say things like, "You think you're bad, you want to control and predict," or he'll say, "How can a man be attracted to you as beautiful as you are, because you act so hard and show no emotions as if you were a man." This vulnerability issue hindered me from initiating sex with my husband at times because I never wanted to feel rejected or be vulnerable with him due to previous hurts or mistrust. Here is where the power of love comes in- my husband is a man's man and borderline male chauvinist so it was hard for me to be vulnerable to him due to that side of him. I felt like the devil would have me lose myself in him. But God is amazing at how He does things. He brings this strong, dominant man into my life who was not scared to be vulnerable and share all his hurts and dysfunctions and would cry and even throw himself under the bus first.He is a man who is not scared to say "I am sorry" if he is wrong, whose main priority is to be on the same page, who stops whatever he is doing to give me his undivided attention because what I have to say is more important than anything else and demands the same respect, who is actually teaching me, through all his dysfunctions how to be vulnerable because, remember, I held on to perfectionism. As my husband challenged me to break all barriers that I put up against vulnerability, I began to challenge myself too, because to know better is to do better. It is not the critic who counts, nor the man or woman who points out how the strong person stumbles or where the doer of deeds could have done them better. The credit belongs to the person who is actually in the arena, whose face is marred by dust, sweat, and blood; who strives valiantly; who errs, who comes short again and again, because there is no effort without error and shortcoming, but who actually strives to do the deeds? Who knows great enthusiasm with great devotions and who spends their time in a worthy cause? Who, at best, knows in the end the triumph of high achievement? Who, at worst, fails, but at least fails while daring greatly. I am learning daily from my great, dysfunctional, vulnerable, strong teacher, my husband, that vulnerability is not a weakness. I am even using the term dysfunctional in a way that shows that his ways may be different than my perfectionist ways, but I'm learning that vulnerability is not knowing victory or defeat, but rather understanding the necessity of both. It's engaging. It's about being all in. The uncertainty, risk, and emotional exposures we face every day are not optional. It is only a question of engagement. Our willingness to own and engage with our vulnerability determines the depth of our courage and the clarity of our purpose. The level to which we protect ourselves from being vulnerable is a measure of our fear and disconnection. If we spend our lives waiting until we're perfect or bulletproof before we walk into the arena, we ultimately sacrifice relationships and opportunities that may not be recoverable.

Bio:

Nicole Valle was born and raised in Philadelphia, Pennsylvania. She graduated from the Philadelphia public school system. After high school graduation, she pursued higher education and attended Cheyney University and majored in biology then transferred to Temple University to complete her nursing degree. Nicole majored in Nephrology nursing and has been in the field for 27 years. Mrs. Valle also had a love for the arts. Her passion for film productions and the arts motivated her to return to school in 2008, where she graduated with her bachelor's in Film Producing and Directing in 2012 from The Art institute of Philadelphia. Nicole has been the CEO of Sunrise Productions LLC since 2000, Nicole is responsible for all the company's productions, including management of events, services & sales.

Facebook: Nicole Valle
Instagram: Sunrise_productions_

Adrien Walker

You Are An Overcomer
By Adrien Walker

On November 23, 2010, my miracle baby and only son was born. It took him a few seconds to take his first breath, but he came into this world as children normally do; kicking and screaming.

I'm not sure if it was the 8 weeks of bedrest, constant monitoring, or in utero condition he had prior to birth, but I had an uneasy feeling. He made it to be over five pounds, which meant no NICU stay, so what was weighing so heavy on my mind?

I was searching for what I would come to know as "genetic markers" or oddities my son was born with. I even went as far as telling my husband that our son was not like the other babies. Sadly, this would prove to be true.

Fast forward to two years later. Two major surgeries and missed milestones, my son was diagnosed with a rare genetic condition called Dup15q. On "diagnosis day," the genetic counselors and developmental pediatricians looked two broken parents in the eyes and told them their only boy would never mentally progress beyond two years of age, would need continuous care his entire life, and would never live up to the vision of the child we had prayed for.

Somehow, we were given the most devastating news that day. He had been diagnosed with the very same disorder I'd found while scouring the internet two years earlier when God had already prepared us for the journey ahead.

I became depressed.

Depression can occur suddenly, or it can be attributed to long suffering that someone learns to incorporate into their normal lives. Women are twice as likely to be affected by depression as men, and it can manifest itself in many ways to include major depression, where you lose the ability to find pleasure in activities once enjoyed; postpartum, occurring after the birth of a baby, and persistent depressive disorder, which is an extended state that lasts for two years or more.

I didn't realize I had been in a numb state of doing all things necessary, yet suffering in a colorless, odorless mental state. "If my son can't have a normal life, then why should I?" This was the lens every thought I had was viewed through. Any dash of joy was fleeting as sorrow loomed.

I am happy to say, as I write these words ten years later, I am an accomplished entrepreneur managing multiple five to six figure businesses and leading a group of like-minded black business owners called the Black Growth Alliance.

The Black Growth Alliance was started in June 2020 as an organization helping prepare black entrepreneurs to compete in the global marketplace by providing educational training opportunities, as well as networking and collaboration. The group quickly grew to over 3,500 members and shows   no signs of slowing down as we are all united with one goal.

My message to other warriors battling depression, grief, "mom-"guilt; please, allow me to share three key reflections that helped me conquer my mental despondency, overcome mediocrity, and live a purpose driven life despite the challenges.

Know that it is okay to put yourself first at times and carry on with your business, hobbies, and things you love. Pursuing your passions provides a much needed outlet and distraction. Giving up on what is inherently "you" will cause resentment. Instead, find time for activities that you enjoy doing.

Set boundaries without guilt in enforcing them. This starts with making a list of non-negotiables and a wiggle list of things that can slip, if necessary, for the greater good.

As an example, your morning spiritual, centering activities are non-negotiables. Whatever you need to start your day and help you run on all cylinders can not go into the "if I have time for it" column. Schedule this time, make it sacred, and let everyone know this is a requirement for your sanctity.

Allow yourself time to process pain, when it enters your mind, in a healthy way. Acknowledge the thought and begin to shift your mindset to the "coming out," like preparing to enter a tunnel of negative thoughts. Go in, go through, and come out. Take more time in the tunnel if necessary, but don't dwell there. There are many tunnels and bridges on the road, so learn how to maneuver them to best serve you on the journey.

Somehow, with no medication or formal help, I put myself back together and rediscovered my passion and zeal for the things I enjoyed. I was not doing my son a disservice by continuing on with my life and carving out time for myself. Rather, I was giving him a more balanced Mom; someone grounded and well equipped to handle our world.

My son gives me snuggles every day and never grows tired of me nuzzling his ear or pulling him in close and smelling his hair. His world is simple, and I get to be a part of all its wonders. Embracing the positives is what propels me to be my best self and enables me to find joy.

Think of that one passion or hobby you have put on the backburner thinking that it's what's expected of being a wife and mom and traversing the rollercoaster of motherhood and life. What's that missing piece of your story?

I pray my story empowers other moms of children with special needs who feel they have lost themselves and can't see past the grief. One day at a time, you will get to the other side.

Bio:
Adrien Walker currently resides in Northern Virginia and is a wife and mother of three children.

Adrien is a sales optimization strategist and helps clients incorporate different monetization methods into their business for maximum profitability.

She is also the founder of the Black Growth Alliance, which is an organization of like-minded black entrepreneurs working together to offer educational opportunities and training sessions, as well as networking and collaboration to help prepare black-owned businesses better compete in the global marketplace.

Adrien has a background in both Real Estate and eCommerce, having sold on various platforms which include Ebay, Amazon, Etsy, and Shopify for over ten years, and she currently owns two six-figure, high-ticket drop shipping stores as well.

To learn more about Adrien, visit her website
BlackGrowthAlliance.org, or search for her Facebook Group, Black
Growth Alliance and @BlackGrowthAlliance on Instagram

Stephanie Wall

G-E-D: Get Everything, God Destined for You !

By Stephanie Wall

"Being realistic is the most common path to mediocrity."
Will Smith

I made the decision. I clicked the button and hit send. As I did , the committee inside my head started whispering, "Are we sure? Do you think we can do this?" " We are doing it!" I committed out loud. I had joined a couple of programs to hone my crafts in writing , speaking, and coaching. Each craft took me outside of my comfort zone in money spent, skills, talents, and abilities. Why is this important? Statistically, individuals with my background rarely accomplish the audacious goals that they set out to achieve . In-fact, not only do they not achieve them, they do not seek success to such a level at all. As a teenage girl raised in poverty and a mother at only 16 years old, there were with few examples of the success I craved. Models unwed, teenage mothers beating the odds with no support were not commonplace in my community.

According to a Career Women's Journal Article dated September 2014, titled "Teen Mothers can become Strong Business Women, "80% of unmarried teen mothers end up on welfare, and only one in three complete high school. Similar studies show that 1.5% of these teenagers gain degrees by the time they are 30." The easiest thing to do would have been to feel sorry for myself and believe that I couldn't have more. I had already crushed mediocrity by obtaining my GED, a bachelor's, and a master's degree from Johns Hopkins University in

Maryland. However, the thought of working for myself and helping others to " crush mediocrity" required me to dig a little deeper and fully "Choose me."

Have you ever decided to do something that you were excited about but too afraid to share with others because of the fear of what they may say, think, or do? If so , welcome to the club. Jonathan Fields, author of the book *"Uncertainty: Turning Fear and Doubt into Fuel for Brilliance,"* suggests that one way to manage our fear or anxiety around new ventures is to develop a plan for the worst possible outcome.

The first step is to conquer the fear of success or failure, depending on how you want to look at it. Either way, I turned to the acronym, F-false-E-evidence-A-appearing-R-real. I learned this from my coach, Jon Talarico in a twelve week program for leaders called "Thinking Into Results," based on 20 years of scientific research through the Proctor Gallagher Institute. This professional and personal development program taught me to ask myself the following questions about my beliefs:

Do I have good, sound reasons for my beliefs?

Where did my beliefs come from?

Would changing my beliefs improve my life?

How do I change my beliefs?

I will not lie to you. It required me to commit to the work. I still worked full-time, along with building my client-base and credibility as a speaker. Imagine this: you work Monday through Friday in a field that you love! You are equally in love with being a speaker, coach , and writer. I know, I know, you are probably saying, "What are you getting done?" I made additional plans to stay focused and make sure that my commitment to my full-time employment did not suffer, and I provided top-notch service to my new clients. Below are some steps that I took. This list is not exhaustive.

- Say "No" to activities that were time wasters or not in line with your goals, full-time employment, or business (this does work)

- Tell your family what you are working on, so they are clear about why you are/or may be unavailable.

- Put everything on a calendar and work off it. I cannot express this enough.

- Do the work !! Do not waste your time or money .

- Practice what you are learning while you are going through the course. It will help you better retain the information.

- Ask questions. Do not be afraid to keep what you need and discard what you do not.

- Work only with the people that you would not mind changing places with.

- Get your rest, ask for help when you need it, and enjoy the journey.

As of this chapter, I have not only increased my skill level in all three areas. I have been a featured speaker on many stages. I have been a part of five book anthologies as a co- author. I have conducted numerous individual and group coaching sessions, as well as incorporated coaching into my talks. I am the visionary behind a book titled "Her story: Our Story Same Trauma Different Faces: True Stories of Triumph." I am the author of the original and second edition of "How My Part-Time Job Saved My Life: A True Story of Overcoming Abuse to Living a Victorious Life."

I am also proud and grateful to have accomplished what I set out to do. Doubt will try to take you off course. Add that fact to your plan for derailment. I reminded myself of what it could be if I succeed and what it would be if I gave up on me . Most of what holds you back from taking chances and growing beyond where you are now is the fear of the unknown. If you have attended college, the military, had children, or gotten married (to name a few), you did so without knowing the outcome.

Now, I challenge you to take a chance on yourself. Write down the things you would do if you were guaranteed success. Then, write down how your life would change if you obtain it. Finally , write down which you would regret not going after as you gain wisdom and years. Get a coach to help to guide you so that you avoid pitfalls. Now, go forth and "crush mediocrity!"

Bio:

Stephanie Wall is a passionate Speaker, Author, and Coach who epitomizes the definition of a purpose-driven life. She is committed to advocating for women survivors of trauma. As a community change-agent who served in law enforcement for 20 years with a master's degree in Business & Organizational Leadership and certifications for Transformational, Solution-based & Life Coaching, she uses empathy and an action-oriented attitude to help people combat life's challenges.

Stephanie authored "How My Part-time Job Saved My Life: A True Story of Overcoming Abuse and Claiming a Victorious Life" to demonstrate how to conquer a traumatic past. Additionally, she is the Co-Author of several of Amazon's #1 Best Sellers books. As a result of her devotion to help women, Stephanie created Speaker Stephanie LLC, a personal development brand bridging her passion and career. From keynote speaking and hosting interactive leadership seminars to individual and group coaching.

Website: Speakerstephanie.com
Instagram: Speakerstephaniew

Dr. Debra Wright Owens

The Winner In Me
By Dr. Debra Wright Owens

I could offer many reasons as an excuse to settle for mediocrity in life, but I decided years ago not to do so . I decided early on that I would pursue the best version of myself, no matter what comes or goes. I wasn't born with a silver spoon in my mouth. Humble beginnings as a native Mississippian taught me the value of hard work, loving God, loving your family and neighbors, and being grateful for the small things in life. We had our challenges as a family, but didn't give it much thought, because so did everyone else in my small hometown. My mother worked her fingers to the bone, to make sure that we had what we needed to survive, and my stepfather did the best he could. I didn't meet my biological father until I was about eleven years old. To this day, he has never explained or apologized for his absence in my life as a child, but I have never held it against him and love him as if he had been there from the beginning. I consider myself blessed to have a relationship with my biological father at all, because some people don't even get that. Remember, I said I'm grateful for the small things too.

Thinking back on my childhood years, I realize that I had a desire to know God as early as seven years old. I clearly remember praying to God for my younger sister when she was just months old. Any time she was ill, I would cry, pray, and ask God to heal her. I remember attending summer bible school at one of the churches in the neighborhood and sitting on the church steps crying, wandering why Jesus was crucified. I regularly attended church while growing up, not because I was forced to go, but because I had a desire to go to church. I

246

had a craving then, and now, as I'm older, I realize that the hand of God has been on my life - all of my life.

As I mentioned, I wasn't born into wealth, but I was indeed born a winner. I have always had an inner drive to excel in life. Settling for mediocrity has never been my normal. This is not to say that I have not had my share of ups and downs. I assure you that I have had both. I have experienced high seasons, enjoying the scenery from the mountain tops. I have also had seasons of being deep down in the valley, those seasons of life that throw a curveball. It is in those valley seasons that we often find ourselves in situations that we never imagined we would be in, and those situations often leave us second-guessing our decisions, purpose, beliefs, values, and even our faith.

When my second marriage ended in 2003, a curve ball that I was not expecting, I was tempted to throw in the towel and just settle for a life of losses. I could have reached back in my childhood archives and offered excuses that I had failed at marriage again because I didn't have a godly marriage example to model after, or I didn't really know my biological father until I was about eleven. I could have decided that my second failed marriage would be my breaking point, but my inner champion would not let it be so! The winner in me refused to lay down and feel sorry for myself from that point forward. Another failed marriage was, indeed, a blow to my hopes and dreams of marriage at that time , but it was not the totality of who I was then, who I would become down the road, or God's purpose and plans for my life. It was not the conclusion of my entire life's story. It was only a chapter. Yes, I was wounded emotionally; weakened and depressed for quite some time, but I fought diligently for my recovery. It took holding on to God with a tighter grip and doing internal work to own my part in two failed marriages. I could not afford to dawdle in self-pity. I had two children who were very young that I had to be strong for. I persevered and found my way back! I would go on to grow in God even more and eventually be ordained as a minister. I finished my master's degree and earned a PhD as well. My children are healthy and productive young adults today. I am pursuing my God-given vision and walking out my life's purpose daily – helping others, because I was born to win!

Some might think that settling for mediocrity is not a big deal and is much easier than putting in the work to win. I beg to differ and want to dispel that thought process. For every excuse anyone can offer to settle for mediocrity, there are even more reasons not to settle. Here's why you can't afford to settle for a life of mediocrity!

- You are living "right now" the only life that you will ever have.

- You were created by the Creator to be creative.

- You were born with an assigned purpose.

- There are people waiting for an impartation of your genius.

- The world is awaiting your unique contribution.

- You are so very extraordinary, that out of approximately 7.5 billion people on earth, there's not one other single person just like you.

- Everything about you is so extremely unique to your individual DNA - you cannot be duplicated.

- Your mind has the capacity to think, dream, envision, and create the extraordinary life that you desire and deserve!

I challenge you to not settle for mediocrity. Rise up, and live your life with purpose as the champion that you are!

Bio:

Dr. Debra Wright Owens, a native Mississippian, is an Empowerment Advocate, Certified Professional Coach, Speaker, Author and Minister, whose God-given purpose is to inform, inspire, and empower individuals to passionately pursue their vision and live life on purpose. She is co-author of the book entitled "Life, Vision, Purpose." She is

Founder and CEO of Encore Empowerment International LLC, a professional service firm that specializes in top tier business and personal development solutions, training and development, and conflict resolution. She is Founder and CEO of The Visionaire Foundation, Inc., a nonprofit, global visionary movement dedicated to enhancing the lives of others through education, knowledge, and selfless service. She is a practicing HR professional with over 33 years of federal service and has earned a PhD in Business Management, a master's in Public Administration and a bachelor's in Criminology. She is a light and positive energy. Dr. Debra has two amazing children, who she truly adores.

WOMEN CRUSHING MEDIOCRITY

Martina Britt Yelverton

What You DON'T Know is Costing You _____!

By #BrandMaster, Martina Britt Yelverton

Who would agree that, on a surface level, "Ignorance is Bliss?" I mean really...

+ Who wants to KNOW the driver of the 18 wheeler behind them is texting?

+ Who wants to KNOW which potluck participant has a cat or an agile dog?

+ Who wants to KNOW that Facebook hears everything, permission or not?

You're probably thinking, "Ah! Me! I'd want to know, so that I can make an informed decision, right? ... Or am I wrong?"

Who has subscribed to the idea that, "Absence makes the heart grow fonder?", or "Money is the root of all evil?"

Lots of us have! But today, with deep consideration, I challenge you to listen even deeper - but not to me - to what YOU feel, see, or hear from yourself.

A very wealthy mentor of mine says, "Note takers are money makers", so I challenge you to write down the ideas that come to YOU - not what I'm saying specifically, but your own thoughts. I am here to tell you that "What you DON'T know is costing you _____!" (you fill in the blank with what YOU see, hear, or feel.)

Let's talk about some areas of daily life around you, that you DON'T know are costing you _____...

1. Friends (offline) - How often do you listen or support in genuine silence instead of solving, nagging or cosigning?

2. Joy & Peace - How often do you suffer in obedience by being in places you are tolerated but not celebrated? Who do you tolerate instead of celebrate?

3. Followers (online) - How often do you find disdain in seeing fight videos, political topics, verbiage of others without reviewing your own timeline to gauge your lack of followers, influence, or shares.

4. Sanity - As a parent, is your sanity challenged because you're too lenient or too strict? How is this causing undue stress and strain on yourself due to your own inconsistencies?

5. Relationships - How many times have you started over without having evaluated your own fault, lack, or behavior?

6. Completion - Perfection is a thief, and completion is a myth.

7. Money - Now, money conversations are not sexy until you have money to talk about, and I mean a lot of it! It gets even sexier when it's paired with a great credit score! Now, add real estate ownership to it, and "She is fine as wine" - right!?

Question...

+ Did you know... that your income is the sum total of your circle of influence?

You do want to make more money, right?

+ Did you know... if you are the smartest person in your circle, you need to get in a new circle?

253

What else do you have to learn there?

+ Do you believe... you know something that others don't?

Of course you do.

+ Do you believe... that you can make money teaching it? You are an expert in something someone else is completely unfamiliar with but wants to learn.

So teach!

Allow me a moment of transparency. I struggled for quite some time with number six: Completion, and #7: Mone..., wait with #5, ...#6, and ...okay, well all of them, but let's stay on topic here. My goal is to have you listen deeper and hear YOUR struggle so you can realize, "What you DON'T know that's costing you _____", and be released from ignorance.

I struggled in and out of four marriages, two to the same man who was my best friend and "dream man." I couldn't understand the communication failures we incurred. I intended to fix my faults from the first time so badly, only to find the same result repeated. Who else missed Maya Angelo's wisdom, that even Oprah echoed:

"When a person shows you who they are, believe them the first time."

I wanted that perfection. All so that I could complete a dream. My next marriage ended due to the devil being busy and domestic violence reared its ugly head. I'd heard enough scenarios where women didn't get a second chance to leave, so that situation was as complete as I needed it to be to leave. I clearly understood Ms. Maya by that time. As for my fourth marriage, while still looking for completion elsewhere and remembering a broken middle school era, I married my middle school protector and best friend. Within months, clearly I knew

I'd repeated a mistake. That decision has taken four years to complete in my head and heart and several trips to the courthouse to finalize.

The lesson I hope you receive for yourself, wherever you may be stuck is to know that everything doesn't have to be complete, or to be over, for YOU to move on for YOU! Don't stay stuck trying to fix what isn't broken in you. If you do that and DON'T know that you're doing it, you're costing yourself _____ .

Pivot with me as I begin to close. Did you know that, as a parent, you grow up with your children? Yes, I know it'd be nice if they realized that too, but I digress. Yes, as a parent, you're STILL growing up yourself! Did you know that your influence as a parent is just as important as the money you struggle to make to provide for your kids?

What if I told you that the frustration you feel about the time you spend away trying to provide for your kids could be made at home with them?

Since we're being forced to work from home if we're lucky, yet on a job we hate and with our loved ones who we are slowly becoming less loving towards. Our kids are being forced to learn online with little to no social interaction. The food and the electric bills keep climbing. While we are pleased to know where our kids are at all times, we simply aren't having any fun. Tensions are high, money is low, credit is getting worse, debt is piling up and fear of job loss is looming.

Since forced virtual solutions are a thing, why not #GetPaidToBeAParent?...

Bio:
Hey yawl! My name is Martina Britt Yelverton, and I am a...

+ BrandMaster

+ CashflowQueen

+ Founder of the #1 Hire Your Kids Legal Tax Hack Movement

My daily goal is to

+ Brand You

+ Educate You &

+ Help You ...#GetYoASSetsInOrder

I am your Go2Girl for Simplified Blueprints & Graphics, and I help people who want help! If you're in need of the help I've been blessed to offer, follow me and select the bell for alerts when I go live on YouTube or Facebook!

FREE CONTENT is available on my Entrepreneurs Secrets Revealed mailing list at http://brandsecretsrevealed.com . Speaking of FREE ... grab your free annual momentum planning tool at: http://momentum.martinabrittyelverton.com

If you've struggled, as a #Parent, as an #Entrepreneur, or as a #Brand or #HomeBasedBusiness owner, I Can Help You:

+ #GetYoASSetsInOrder

+ #Get Branded

+ #Get Found On Google

+ #Get Paid Daily &

+ #Get Published on Amazon

If you're serious, text "brandmaster" to 474747 TODAY!